The Lost
Birds of Paradise

EPIMACHUS ELLIOTI.

J. Wolf. & J. Smit del. et lith.

M & N. Hanhart imp

The Lost
Birds of Paradise

ERROL FULLER

SWAN·HILL
PRESS

For Elsie Fuller

First published in the UK in 1995
by Swan Hill Press
an imprint of Airlife Publishing Ltd

British Library Cataloguing in Publication Data
A catalogue record for this book
is available from the British Library

ISBN 1 85310 566 X

Printed in Singapore

Swan Hill Press
an imprint of Airlife Publishing Ltd
101 Longden Road, Shrewsbury SY3 9EB

TABLE OF CONTENTS

LIST OF COLOUR PLATES

LIST OF BLACK AND WHITE ILLUSTRATIONS

Preface

The heyday of plume-hunting dawned with the middle years of the reign of Queen Victoria and closed with the onset of World War I. During those years unimaginable numbers of birds were slaughtered for their plumes – chiefly to satisfy the whims of the fashion industry and, most particularly, its millineries. No group of birds suffered a more intense persecution than the birds of paradise; thousands died each year on account of their exquisite plumes. The countless crates of trade skins shipped from New Guinea to Europe and North America almost always contained bundle after bundle of familiar sorts, but on very rare occasions something quite unexpected would come to light – an individual of a kind not seen before. Sometimes a decade or more might pass before a similar bird was identified, sometimes no other was ever found and the skin, with its plumes attached, remained unique. Usually, these anomalous discoveries found their way into museums – public or private – where they remain still shrouded in mystery, lying in darkened drawers or perched upon dusty shelves. With the decline in plume-hunting, most have never been encountered again.

These are the lost birds of paradise.

Plate I
The Lost Birds of Paradise – sixteen birds discovered during the heyday of plume hunting. Top row (from left): Mantou's Rifle Bird; Duivenbode's Rifle Bird; Sharpe's Lobe-billed Rifle Bird; Rothschild's Lobe-billed Bird of Paradise. Second row: Astrapian Sicklebill; Elliot's Bird of Paradise; Duivenbode's Six-wired Bird of Paradise; Wilhelmina's Bird of Paradise. Third row: King of Holland's Bird of Paradise; Lyre-tailed King; Ruys' Bird of Paradise; Bensbach's Bird of Paradise. Bottom row: Wonderful Bird of Paradise; Lupton's Bird of Paradise; Frau Reichenow's Bird of Paradise; 'Paradisea mixta'.

Introduction

When the *Vittoria* straggled into the harbour of Seville in September 1522, she appeared as a ship sailing from a nightmare and her crew – worn, half-starved and sickly – seemed as men returned from the dead. The ship's sails were in tatters, the timbers and boards were holed and the masts splintered. This wretched craft was the remnant of five splendid sailing vessels that had proudly set sail from Seville more than three years earlier under the leadership of Ferdinand Magellan.

The aim of their voyage was to reach the Spice Islands by sailing west rather than east and thus, by continuing on home in the same direction, eventually to circumnavigate the globe. Misadventure, illness and hardship turned this fine adventure into a disaster for those who participated in it. Out of 277 men who had set sail, only nineteen completed the round trip; Magellan himself was hacked to death in the Philippines before the Spice Islands themselves had even been reached. But despite the distressed state of both ship and crew, the *Vittoria* was loaded with a rich store of treasure brought back from the epic journey.

Among the wonders carried from the ship's hold were several fantastically coloured bird skins decorated with long, delicate, lace-like plumes – a gift to the captain of the *Vittoria* from the Sultan of Batjan who had received them from a far-off land to the south of his own island. Crudely preserved and dried by native hunters, the feet and flesh of each bird had been removed during the preservation process and from this simple, practical act grew a legend that blossomed for centuries.

Figure 1
(Left), Wallace's Standard-winged Bird of Paradise (*Semioptera wallacii*) – males above and below left, female below right. Hand-coloured lithograph by J. Wolf and J. Smit from D.G. Elliot's *Monograph of the Paradiseidae* (London, 1873).

Figure 2
(Right), Wilson's Bird of Paradise (*Diphyllodes respublica*) – males above left and below, female above right. Hand-coloured lithograph by J. Gould and W. Hart from J. Gould's *Birds of New Guinea* (London, 1875–88).

INTRODUCTION

From where could these exquisite creatures have come – birds without flesh and with no means of alighting on land, carried to Europe on a ship from hell? Only one answer appears to have satisfied the emotional needs of a sixteenth-century public. Being without feet the birds could never have alighted on ground or tree, being without flesh they were incapable of decay and needed no bodily sustenance; they were weightless, ethereal creatures of the upper airs. They were birds from Paradise.

These first specimens are now believed to have been of the species *Paradisea minor* (Lesser Bird of Paradise) but other quite different, yet clearly related, birds were soon brought back to Europe by ships voyaging in the wake of Magellan.

As European influence and power extended – and it became established that these creatures came not from Paradise but instead from the mysterious island of New Guinea – so it became realised that these gorgeously attired birds came in many different shapes and sizes. Gradually – and the process took more than 400 years – the remarkable diversity of the birds of paradise was revealed to European explorers and naturalists.

At a superficial level the many species within this extravagant bird family may betray little sign of their relationship to one another. Some have long, flowing tails, others rather short, stumpy ones; some are small, dainty birds, others larger and more hulking, often looking like great coloured crows. Some have long, slender, sickle-shaped bills, others have beaks that are short, stubby and straight. There are birds of paradise with gloriously coloured plumes or with striking breast plates made up of glowing metallic-looking feathers of blue or green; others are decorated with feather fans, great capes or ruffs, head or tail wires, or wattles of red, blue or yellow.

This great diversity of plumage is shown mostly by the males; it is the female birds that clearly demonstrate the cohesion of the group. Although their respective partners may differ in every conceivable plumage characteristic, females of the various species can be strikingly similar to one another in appearance. Characteristically, they show none of the more outrageous ornamental plumage but instead are quietly dressed in browns and greys often with delicate barring on their underparts.

Figure 3
(Left), Black-billed Sicklebill
(*Drepanornis albertisii*) – female left,
male right. Hand-coloured
lithograph by J. Gould and W. Hart
from J. Gould's *Birds of New Guinea*
(London, 1875–88).

Figure 4
(Right), King of Saxony's Bird of
Paradise (*Pteridophora alberti*) – male.
Hand-coloured lithograph by W.
Hart from R. Bowdler Sharpe's
Monograph of the Paradiseidae
(London, 1891–8).

Plate II
Lesser Bird of Paradise (*Paradisea minor*). Watercolour by Jacques Barraband (1745–1809).

Although a few species occur in the Moluccas and in eastern Australia, the true home of the birds of paradise is the great island of New Guinea, now politically divided into two – Irian Jaya in the west, Papua in the east. Just over forty species are currently recognised, some of these comparatively well known, others less so. What is not generally realised is the fact that there remain more than twenty additional –

Plate III
Red Bird of Paradise (*Paradisea rubra*). Watercolour by Jacques Barraband (1745–1809).

and quite distinct – forms, the exact status of each of which is obscure and in many cases has never been satisfactorily determined.

These mysterious birds of paradise show one uniting feature: exceptional scarcity. Mostly, they are known only from isolated museum specimens, usually of some age, that lack any precise locality data. In the majority of cases they have been known since

Figure 5
(Left), Lionel Walter Rothschild,
2nd Baron Rothschild of Tring
(1868–1937). Courtesy of The Hon.
Miriam Rothschild.

Figure 6
(Right), Professor Erwin Stresemann
(1889–1972).

the years before World War I when New Guinea belonged, in name at least, to three of the great colonial powers – Holland, Germany and Britain – and plume-hunting was at its height. Coming to attention almost exclusively as a result of the plume trade, most have not been encountered since its end and only a very few have been found by ornithologists on their own home grounds.

Almost all were originally considered legitimate species and their discovery and initial description tended to follow the same pattern. An unusual trade skin, probably bartered from native hunters, would fall into the hands of a merchant capable of appreciating its rarity. It would be forwarded by him – as a considerable, and appropriately priced, treasure – to an eminent naturalist or great museum. At its destination it would be pounced upon by the ablest ornithologists of the period, all anxious to be first into print with a description of any new species. The number of unusual, or even unique, skins that may have fallen through this particular net and ended up as hat decorations or fashion accessories can only be guessed at; many rare plumes were perhaps lost for ever as a hat aged or modes changed.

As the golden age of ornithological discovery drew to a close some sixty bird of paradise species were recognised, approximately one third more than are listed today. By the year 1930 it had come to be realised that these sixty species could be fitted into two broad categories: those that had been seen by ornithologists in the wild and those that had not. This realisation had already led to a certain amount of suspicion regarding the status of some of these 'lost' birds. Might it not be, some commentators argued, that a number of them were simply hybrids between the better known species? Assuming the production of hybrids to be an uncommon occurrence, this would account for the extreme rarity of specimens. The suspicion was supported by the undeniable fact that some of the 'lost' birds showed what might be termed 'intermediate' plumage characteristics.

In the year 1930 the German ornithologist Erwin Stresemann conducted a review

Figure 7
A nineteenth-century cartoon
published in the magazine *Punch*.
Lampooning the fashion for wearing
feathers, it was captioned 'A Bird of
Prey'.

of all the bird of paradise 'species' whose home grounds remained unknown. His con-
tention was that all of these, not just some, were hybrids. At this time there were
perhaps two great names in bird of paradise research. One was Stresemann himself,
the other was Lionel Walter Rothschild, 2nd Baron Rothschild of Tring. Lionel
Rothschild, or Walter as he came to be called, was an avid natural history collector
with a special interest in, and an unparalleled collection of, birds of paradise. In addition to creating his own museum and sponsoring collectors and explorers the world
over, Rothschild had founded his own zoological journal, *Novitates Zoologicae*. It was
to Rothschild and his journal that Stresemann turned when he wished to publish the
findings of his research. This was a fairly natural development for it was only with
Rothschild's co-operation that Stresemann had been able to pursue his investigation;
Walter held the key to the entire enterprise – he owned more than half of the specimens that Stresemann needed to study!

Accordingly, *Welche Paradiesvogelarten der Literatur sind Hybriden Ursprungs?*
appeared in *Novitates Zoologicae* for 1930. In this paper, published in German,

Stresemann proposed a hybrid origin for each kind of bird of paradise known only from museum specimens. Without any regard for matters of doubt or consideration of the possibility of error, with no outlining of the range of possibilities or, indeed, any detailed discussion of the actual evidence, Stresemann named specific parents – chosen from among the more familiar bird of paradise species – for each cryptic form.

Stresemann's reputation was such that his findings went largely unchallenged. How thoroughly his paper, written in German, was scrutinised by his contemporaries cannot now be determined, but in the decades that have passed since its publication few ornithologists have commented upon it. Today, most naturalists are unaware of the lost birds of paradise. Among those who do know of them, there is a fairly general assumption – not usually based on any examination of the specimens or, in fact, of Stresemann's text – that they have been satisfactorily accounted for. With the specimens themselves now scattered among museums spread throughout the world, the practical problems involved in attempting to conduct a critical or comparative survey are not inconsiderable. Perhaps for this reason, most writers who have produced studies of the Paradiseidae make little comment on the alleged hybrids. Gilliard (1969), for instance, lists them, indicates a limited dissatisfaction with the hybrid hypothesis but does not review the mysterious forms in any depth; Forshaw, in Cooper and Forshaw (1977), fails to mention them at all; Coates (1990) briefly and accurately notes those species that are thought to have crossed. Only Iredale (1950), in a wildly eccentric book, examines them in detail.

There can be little doubt that, in the majority of cases, Stresemann's diagnoses are correct. Built around telling plumage characteristics and geographical possibility, they are, for the most part, thorough exercises in deduction. In a few instances, however, Stresemann's enthusiasm for his own idea and his evident desire to tie together all the loose ends of the mystery, lead him away from firm ground. In these instances, he speculates. There is nothing wrong with speculation, of course; the problem with Stresemann's paper is that he makes no distinction between informed guesswork and clear evidence. Regrettably, later writers have reported all his designations as if they were proven.

In a number of cases there is simply not enough clear evidence to justify any definitive solution. Several lost birds of paradise appear to have been relegated to hybrid status largely as a result of others being demonstrably of such an origin. Even if these forms are truly hybrids, they may not be the particular hybrids stated. Species other than those suggested can, with equal justification, be put forward as putative parents. Certainly, Stresemann paid little attention to ethological considerations. In the light of current knowledge there is no final solution to all of the problems posed by the lost birds of paradise. The majority are certainly hybrids. Some others seem likely to be so. A few may constitute valid species, species that are now either extinct or that cling to survival in an inaccessible or overlooked locality somewhere in the formidable wilderness that is New Guinea.

It might be supposed that DNA testing techniques could resolve any elements of doubt surrounding the status of these birds. Unfortunately, however, this discipline, in as far as it relates to birds, is not yet as well established as might be imaged. The closer the relationship of the putative parents to one another, the less reliable any results would be. Testing the lost birds of paradise would involve particular problems.

Figure 8
Mysterious New Guinea. This rather eerie photograph of a 'spirit house' was taken by H. Meyer during the 1920s.

They are, of course, scattered around the world and, perhaps more crucially, any testing would, of necessity, have to be carried out on specimens of considerable age. No fresh tissue would be available. Owners of specimens may not be prepared to allow them to be hacked about, or otherwise tampered with, in order to secure samples. Perhaps equally important is the fact that these birds have been largely forgotten. No one is likely to invest money in testing them (and the cost would be considerable) until more interest is generated. At the present time, the application of DNA testing to the problem of the lost birds of paradise – and any conclusions produced – would be as open to criticism as more traditional evaluations of evidence.

Since the time of Stresemann's writing a few additional anomalous forms have come to the ornithological world's attention. Like those known only from the era of the plume trade, these birds are surrounded by an aura of mystery. They show that the process of discovery begun so long ago by Magellan's men is still ongoing and that, perhaps, the last secrets of the birds of paradise will never be prised from the steamy lowland forests and mountain jungles of New Guinea.

The Lost
Birds of Paradise

MANTOU'S RIFLE BIRD

Seleucidis melanoleuca × *Ptiloris magnificus*

Craspedophora mantoui Oustalet, 1891, *Le Naturaliste*, 13, p.260.
Craspedophora bruijni Büttikofer, 1894, *Notes Leyden Museum*, 16, p.161.
Heteroptilorhis mantoui Sharpe, 1893, *Monograph of the Paradiseidae*, p.X.
Seleucidis melanoleuca × *Ptiloris magnificus* Suchetet, 1897, *Des Hybrides à l'État Sauvage*,
    p.420

DESCRIPTION

Purplish black above with purplish violet glossing to velvety black-tipped feathers; wing coverts velvet black glossed with steel blue; primaries black edged with purple; tail velvet black glossed purple but centre feathers glossed steel blue; crown metallic green; sides of face and upper throat purplish violet; lower throat steel green, united to breast shield of metallic blue crinkled feathers that show a purplish gloss, the lateral feathers of this shield being black with a steel green margin; rest of breast and abdomen reddish purple with bronze reflections and separated from breast shield by narrow band of golden bronze; filamentous flank plumes with purple gloss; tuft of white feathers on thighs.

MEASUREMENTS

Length 280 mm (11 inches); wing 185 mm; tail 90 mm; bill 66 mm; tarsus 46 mm.

PLACE OF ORIGIN

North-west New Guinea.

LOCATION OF SPECIMENS

Berlin, Leiden, London (Tring) – two specimens, New York – five specimens, Paris.

Nouvelles Archives du Muséum 3ᵉ Sèrie

Mémoires T. IV. Pl. 15.

Craspedophora Mantoui (Oust.)

G. Masson Editeur

Stᵉ des Imp. Lemercier, Paris.

Plate IV
Mantou's Rifle Bird. Hand-coloured
lithograph by J.G. Keulemans from
Nouvelle Archives de Muséum, Paris
(1892), Pl.15.

Mantou's Rifle Bird

Monsieur Suchetet, in his zeal for the discovery of hybrids in a state of nature, has fallen foul of the present bird, and actually suggests the possibility of its being a hybrid between *Craspedophora magnifica* [Magnificent Rifle Bird] and *Seleucidis nigricans* [Twelve-wired Bird of Paradise]. This is certainly one of the most extraordinary propositions ever conceived in the history of ornithology.

With the vigour that characterises much nineteenth-century ornithological writing, Richard Bowdler Sharpe, author of the sumptuous and celebrated double-volume *Monograph of the Paradiseidae* (1891–8), defended the status of the bird he called *Heteroptilorhis mantoui* – Mantou's Rifle Bird.

Even while Bowdler Sharpe was painstakingly compiling his influential work, the nature of this puzzling form was obviously causing discussion. Such is the ambiguity of the bird's plumage that it appears to have aroused suspicion long before other cryptic birds of paradise began to do so. Given this background of early controversy, perhaps it is hardly surprising that a specimen of Mantou's Rifle Bird eventually provided the impetus for Dr Erwin Stresemann, one-time Director of the Berlin Museum, to begin work on the influential paper, *Welche Paradiesvogelarten der Literatur sind Hybriden Ursprungs?* (1930), that effectively relegated all problematical birds of paradise to hybrid status.

Ten examples of this aberrant rifle bird are known, and at one time no less than seven of these were the property of Walter Rothschild. His vast natural history collection, housed in a purpose-built museum at Tring in Hertfordshire, was rich in many ornithological areas and birds of paradise were particularly well represented. The museum was ultimately bequeathed to the British people (part of it now forming the BMNH's sub-department of ornithology) but, rather sadly, perhaps, the birds of paradise were not part of the bequest, having been sold to the American Museum of Natural History in New York some years before Rothschild's death.

During the year 1929 Rothschild, probably feeling that his share of the known specimens of Mantou's Rifle Bird was a trifle extravagant, decided to reduce his holding to six. Consequently, he included a specimen in an exchange with the Berlin Museum where it immediately came to the attention of Dr Stresemann. Like Monsieur Suchetet before him, Stresemann noticed plumage characteristics 'intermediate' between the Twelve-wired Bird of Paradise (*Seleucidis melanoleuca*) and the Magnificent Rifle Bird (*Ptiloris magnificus*) and, convinced by these of the hybrid nature of Berlin's recent acquisition, he pursued his hypothesis until he felt able to shelter beneath its umbrella every 'rare' bird of paradise then known.

Whatever the merit of his argument in other cases, there seems little reason to suppose Stresemann anything but correct in this instance – notwithstanding Bowdler Sharpe's bold stand to the contrary. It was Stresemann's belief that Mantou's Rifle Bird appeared much as one might expect a cross between the Magnificent Rifle Bird and the Twelve-wired Bird of Paradise to appear, and on this rather subjective decision he rested his case. Although this by no means represents conclusive proof of hybridisation, evidence has subsequently come to light that goes much of the way to confirm-

ill & Fox.

British Birds
Vol III Pl 13

Born Nov. 22ⁿᵈ 1847 Died Dec. 25ᵗʰ 1909.

Figure 9
Richard Bowdler Sharpe
(1847–1909), English naturalist and
author of *Monograph of the
Paradiseidae* (London, 1891–8).

Plate V
Magnificent Rifle Bird (*Ptiloris magnificus*) – male above, female below. Hand-coloured lithograph by J. Gould and W. Hart from J. Gould's *Birds of New Guinea* (London, 1875–88), Pl.13.

Plate VI
(Opposite), Twelve-wired Bird of Paradise (*Seleucidis melanoleuca*) – male above, female below. Hand-coloured lithograph by J. Wolf and J. Smit from D. G. Elliot's *Monograph of the Paradiseidae* (London, 1873), Pl.22.

ing Stresemann's supposition. It is generally believed that the two putative parents are closely related, even though the respective males of the species do not greatly resemble one another (by contrast, the females are quite similar). More telling than this closeness of relationship, however, is the fact that female Magnificent Rifle Birds have actually been observed at the displays of male Twelve-wired Birds of Paradise (*see* Coates, 1990). In the light of these observations it is difficult to believe that 'mistakes' are not sometimes made and, assuming this to be the case, it seems probable that the fruits of such matings include the ten anomalous specimens listed as Mantou's Rifle Bird.

These specimens all came with no locality data at all or else with data of only the vaguest kind – north-west New Guinea! As most plume-hunting did, in fact, occur

J. Wolf & J. Smit del et lith   M & N Hanhart imp

SELEUCIDES ALBA

in western New Guinea, the locality data is perhaps of little significance. Assuming the hybrid hypothesis to be correct it is likely that Mantou's Bird will occur not only in the north-west but wherever the parent species come into contact – much of south-east New Guinea for instance. Both alleged parents are birds of the lowland, and vast tracts of country represent 'shared' territory.

The type specimen was a plumassier's skin that was acquired, in 1891, by a Paris dealer, Monsieur Mantou. Mantou generously presented his then unique bird to the Paris Museum, in recognition of which act the 'species' was promptly named in his honour. One of the other nine specimens, the one now at the Leiden Museum, was alleged to be quite distinct and given the name *Craspedophora bruijni* by J. Büttikofer in 1894. Later researchers have been unable to accept that there are any significant differences between this example and the others.

Figure 10
The Tring Museum at the end of the nineteenth century. Courtesy of The Hon. Miriam Rothschild.

Figure 11
Part of the interior of Rothschild's museum – a photograph giving some insight into the scale of his collection. Courtesy of The Hon. Miriam Rothschild.

DUIVENBODE'S RIFLE BIRD

Paryphephorus duivenbodei Meyer, 1890

Craspedophora duivenbodei Meyer, 1890, *Ibis*, p.419.
Paryphephorus duivenbodei Meyer, 1890, *Ibis*, p.420.
Ptilorbis magnifica × *Lophorina superba* Stresemann, 1930, *Novitates Zoologicae* 36, p.11.

DESCRIPTION

Dresden specimen: general colour velvet black with purplish gloss; crown metallic green; sides of face and throat black with purple and bronze reflections; hindneck black with fan-like frill of black feathers glossed violet; triangular breast shield of metallic green showing more blue towards margins; tail black with two central feathers metallic steel green; underparts black with bronze and violet washing on flanks.
British Museum specimen: general colour velvet black with purplish gloss; crown metallic blue and purple; sides of face black with slight golden olive tinge; throat black giving way to shield of metallic blue green that begins very narrowly one inch below base of bill and widens on breast to terminate in a purplish band; rest of underparts black; back (showing no significant cape), wings and tail black with tail glossed blue; iris (according to Shaw Mayer) dark brown; bill, legs and feet black.

MEASUREMENTS

Dresden specimen: length 240 mm (9½ inches); wing 165 mm; tail 98 mm; bill 42 mm; tarsus 38 mm.
New York specimen: wing 151 mm; tail 93mm; bill 40 mm; tarsus 38 mm.

PLACE OF ORIGIN

Deva Deva and Foula – mountain locations inland from Yule Island.

LOCATION OF SPECIMENS

Dresden (destroyed or lost), London (Tring), New York.

Plate VII
Duivenbode's Rifle Bird. Hand-coloured lithograph by J.G. Keulemans from the *Ibis* (1890), Pl.12.

Ibis. 1890. Pl. XII.

$\frac{2}{5}$

Duivenbode's Rifle Bird

Even among the lost birds of paradise, Duivenbode's Rifle Bird stands out as a particularly mysterious form, despite the fact that, unlike most others, it has actually been encountered by ornithologists in the wild. Three examples exist, or have existed, in museum collections, but the precise relationship of the first of these – which apparently no longer survives – to the other two is not certain. A single trade skin first aroused the attention of naturalists to this aberrant rifle bird, but two remarkably similar, yet not quite identical, individuals have subsequently been seen – and collected – by field ornithologists either at, or very close to, the birds' home grounds.

At the beginning of the last decade of the nineteenth century, an unusual preserved skin without proper locality data passed through the hands of Messrs van Duivenbode, Dutch merchants at Ternate, on its way to the Dresden Museum, an institution at this time fast establishing a formidable reputation for ornithological research. From Dresden it was described as the type specimen of a new species – *Craspedophora* (later changed to *Paryphephorus*) *duivenbodei* – by A.B. Meyer. The specimen was painted by the great ornithological illustrator J.G. Keulemans, and this picture was reproduced to accompany Meyer's description in the *Ibis* for 1890. Regrettably, the skin seems to have been a casualty of the fire-bombing of Dresden during the later stages of World War II; certainly Siegfried Eck of the Staatliches Museum für Tierkunde felt unable to confirm its continuing existence, despite the fact that other rare birds of paradise remain at Dresden intact. This represents a significant loss, especially as this particular individual showed an important feature – a pronounced cape of black feathers on the upper back – lacking in the two birds subsequently associated with it.

During the month of July 1903, a collecting expedition undertaken by Antwerp Edgar Pratt and his son Harry encountered an apparently similar bird at Foula (a location inland from Yule Island, some twenty miles west of Mount Albert Edward) in what was then British New Guinea. This specimen, taken at an altitude of 4,000 feet (1,300 metres), was acquired by Walter Rothschild and eventually passed to the American Museum of Natural History along with the rest of Rothschild's bird of paradise collection. No further examples being forthcoming, the species *Paryphephorus duivenbodei* came under attack, and when Erwin Stresemann reviewed all rare birds of paradise in 1930 he considered it to be the hybrid of the Magificent Rifle Bird (*Ptiloris magnificus*) and the Superb Bird of Paradise (*Lophorina superba*).

Seven years after Stresemann's paper was published another, quite unexpected, example of Duivenbode's Rifle Bird was found. On 1 November 1937, the celebrated bird collector Fred Shaw Mayer was working in south-east New Guinea, his precise location being the mountains inland from Yule Island. Here, by Deva Deva (no more than a mile or two from Pratt's camp at Foula), at an altitude of 5,000 feet (1,600 metres), a native collector brought him the third specimen of *Paryphephorus duivenbodei*, an example now in the British Museum (Natural History) collection (reg. no. 1939. 11. 7. 1). Like Pratt's bird, Shaw Mayer's also lacks any distinct cape of black feathers on the upper back.

The circumstance of this individual being found so close to the locality where the

1903 bird was collected is, of course, unlikely to be just coincidence. Either a marked area of overlap between the two proposed parent species exists here – this hybrid zone being tapped in both 1903 and 1937 – or *Paryphephorus duivenbodei* is a legitimate species with a very restricted range in the mountains of south-east New Guinea. Both interpretations have their attractions. In a very broad manner Duivenbode's Rifle Bird might be considered intermediate between the Magnificent Rifle Bird and the Superb Bird of Paradise, but these are generalised connections rather than specific ones. All three kinds are black, they all have bluish green metallic breast shields, and the original *duivenbodei* (although not the two subsequent finds) has a black cape that quite possibly indicates the interaction of the Superb Bird. On these kind of grounds, however, one could argue for a hybrid origin for several quite legitimate bird of paradise species were they known only from museum specimens. Wahnes' Six-wired Bird of Paradise (*Parotia wahnesi*), for instance, might, on account of its long tail, be considered a cross between another six-wired species and an *Astrapia*.

An element that muddles the picture still further, of course, is the lack of a distinct cape (the most dramatic intermediate feature) on the two surviving specimens. Exactly what this lack indicates is unclear. Not only can there now be no direct comparison of specimens, it is almost certain that no such comparison ever took place.

Another puzzling consideration concerns the locality at which the alleged hybrids are known to occur. Both of the supposed parents, the Magnificent Rifle Bird and the Superb Bird of Paradise, are species that range across much of New Guinea. If they

Figure 12
(Left), J.G. Keulemans (1842–1912), the most prolific, and probably the most skilled, ornithological illustrator of his day.

Figure 13
(Right), Antwerp Edgar Pratt, author of *Two Years Among New Guinea Cannibals* (1906) and discoverer of the second specimen of Duivenbode's Rifle Bird.

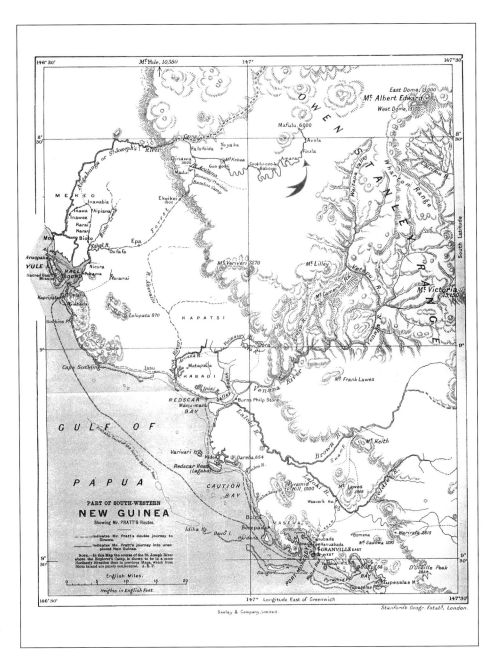

Plate VIII
Pratt's map of his journey into
unexplored territory. Foula is
marked with a red arrow. Deva
Deva, although unmarked, is within
a mile or two of this spot.

do hybridise, their offspring might be expected to turn up anywhere rather than in just one quite specific area. This may, of course, actually be happening; assuming Duivenbode's Rifle Bird to be a comparatively rare hybrid it would, understandably, be easily overlooked in the field. On the other hand, two specimens found in the same area and none definitely known to come from elsewhere (the type specimen of *duivenbodei* lacked locality data) is, statistically, quite suggestive. Even from this information, though, no real conclusion can be reached. Although in a generalised sense the ranges of the putative parent species overlap in much of New Guinea, their altitudinal preferences tend to exclude the likelihood of contact. The Magnificent Rifle Bird is normally found to heights of 3,500 feet (1,200 metres) and the Superb Bird between heights of 5,000 feet (1,600 metres) and 6,000 feet (1,900 metres), limits that are very approximate with both species being prepared to venture a little outside

34

Plate IX
(Above, left), The breast shield of
Duivenbode's Rifle Bird.

Plate X
(Above, right), Duivenbode's Rifle
Bird (upper parts).

Plate XI
(Left), Shaw Mayer's specimen,
collected during 1937 in the
mountains inland from Yule Island.

them. Perhaps there are special circumstances operating in the mountains of south-east New Guinea that bring these birds into more regular contact. If, however, the plumage evidence for hybridisation is regarded as unconvincing, the issue becomes quite straightforward: the species *Paryphephorus duivenbodei* has been found twice in the mountains inland from Yule Island simply because that is where it lives.

Figure 14
Wahnes' Six-wired Bird of Paradise
(*Parotia wahnesi*). Hand-coloured
lithograph by H. Grönvold from the
Ibis (1911).

New Guinea very obviously represents a formidable wilderness still capable of springing zoological surprises. Very recently, for instance, a large and hitherto unknown black and white tree kangaroo was discovered in the central mountains. Yet the concept of a lost, and very beautiful, bird of paradise species within a hundred miles of the Papuan capital Port Moresby might seem a little extravagant. Perhaps Duivenbode's Rifle Bird is a hybrid after all.

Figure 15
The Owen Stanley Mountains,
south-east New Guinea. The home
of a lost bird of paradise?

SHARPE'S LOBE-BILLED RIFLE BIRD

Parotia sefilata × *Paradigalla carunculata?*

Loborhamphus ptilorhis Sharpe, 1908, *Bulletin of the British Ornithologists' Club*, 11, p.67.
Parotia sefilata × *Paradigalla carunculata* Stresemann, 1930, *Novitates Zoologicae, 36,*
    p.12.

DESCRIPTION
Crown metallic violet; rest of head black with tuft of black feathers above bill and patch of iridescent green behind tuft; chin dark green merging into black of throat, this black gradually shading into disintegrated breast plate of metallic pink, turquoise and violet; lower breast black, followed by barring of cream and chocolate brown on flanks and abdomen; back velvet black with some green shimmer; wings and tail black giving off violet hue in some lights; small fleshy wattle at gape.

MEASUREMENTS
Length 330 mm (13 inches); wing 180 mm; tail 157 mm; bill 33 mm; tarsus 53 mm.

PLACE OF ORIGIN
Dutch New Guinea.

LOCATION OF SPECIMEN
London (Tring).

Plate XII
Sharpe's Lobe-billed Rifle Bird. Oil painting by Mark Twombley.

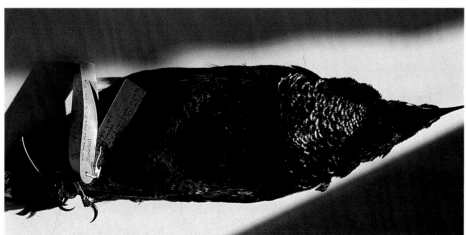

Plate XIII
The type specimen of *Loborhamphus ptilorhis*.

Sharpe's Lobe-Billed Rifle Bird

In 1908 a rather ungainly, perhaps not quite mature, black bird of paradise, illuminated with a confusing yet somehow incomplete array of sheens, glosses and iridescence and carrying an almost imperceptible wattle, was purchased by the British Museum from one D.K. Dunstall. Its registration number at the Museum is 1908. 4. 10. 1 and its place of origin Dutch New Guinea. Richard Bowdler Sharpe promptly published a description and named the bird *Loborhamphus ptilorhis* – the Lobe-billed Rifle Bird. Little of substance can be added to these bare facts. No similar bird has ever been identified; the type specimen remains unique.

An undefinable lack of purity in the plumage suggests the bird may be a hybrid but such impressions are, of course, highly subjective. If the hybrid idea is pursued it becomes difficult to specify which two species could be responsible. Several combinations can be put forward, each, perhaps, with as much validity, and as many drawbacks, as the next. Even Erwin Stresemann, with his capacity for tidying up all the loose ends of paradise bird systematics, made out an indifferent case. He proposed that Sharpe's *Loborhamphus ptilorhis* was the progeny of the Long-tailed Paradigalla (*Paradigalla carunculata*) and the Arfak Six-wired Bird of Paradise (*Parotia sefilata*). This hypothesis is not at variance with the 'Dutch New Guinea' locality, involves species that might meet in parts of their respective ranges, and is not a combination used to account for any other problematical form. Beyond that, the evidence in support of it is a little lukewarm.

At a very general level the unique type specimen conforms roughly with what might be expected in such a cross, but there are no incontrovertible marks of it; indeed Sharpe, in giving the name *Loborhamphus ptilorhis*, had pointed directly to a resemblance to the rifle birds. Stresemann's discussion of the morphology of the mysterious bird is as perplexing as the bird itself. He suggests that it has characteristics of both chosen parents, lists none of these, then points out features not present in either alleged parent but existing in a completely different genus (violet colouring of wing and tail resembling male *Astrapia*, barring on flanks and abdomen resembling female).

Although this analysis is unsatisfactory, it is difficult to give more clarity to the issue. It might be said that the Lobe-billed Rifle Bird and its suggested parents are roughly alike in size, but this is hardly helpful. The beak is like that of *Paradigalla*, a similarity made quite apparent by the presence of a nasal tuft and an exposed flap of skin (this is really no more than a lobing of the gape, however, and is quite unlike Paradigalla's much more developed multicoloured wattling). In shape the tail is similar to that of the Six-wired Bird (the only previously published illustration – in Iredale, 1950 – wrongly shows the tail as long and pointed) but this is not a very clear indicator. A positive affinity with the Six-wired might be the breast shield, but even here it is difficult to draw conclusions as the shield is incomplete, perhaps due to immaturity, in the putative hybrid.

The relationship of the two suggested parent species is not considered to be particularly close, and from the little that is known of the habits of these birds it cannot be said that pairing between them seems particularly likely. This very distance, however, may ultimately help to resolve the enigma; certainly it would make the results of any future DNA testing conducted on Sharpe's Lobe-bill easier to interpret. Perhaps such techniques will soon be sophisticated enough to either confirm or refute Stresemann's hypothesis. For the time being *Loborhamphus ptilorhis* remains a mystery. *Paradigalla carunculata* × *Parotia sefilata* is simply the best guess.

ROTHSCHILD'S LOBE-BILLED BIRD OF PARADISE

Loborhamphus nobilis Rothschild, 1901

Loborhamphus nobilis Rothschild, 1901, *Bulletin of the British Ornithologists' Club*, 12, p.34.

Paradigalla carunculata × *Lophorina superba* Stresemann, 1930, *Novitates Zoologicae*, 36, p.12.

DESCRIPTION

Crown purple; chin bearded, coloured dark bronze green; rest of head and sides of neck black glossed with reddish violet; neck, back and rump velvety black, glossed bronze; wings and tail black with some purplish sheen; throat dark bronze green; breast glittering purple with metallic blue shimmer and with lateral tufts bordered with metallic blue; lower breast shows ill-defined bronze green band; rest of underparts black washed purple; bill and legs black; two yellow fleshy folds forming short wattles around basal third of bill.

MEASUREMENTS

Length 300 mm (12 inches); wing 159–161 mm; tail 146 mm; bill 35–37 mm; tarsus 41–43 mm.

PLACE OF ORIGIN

Dutch New Guinea.

Plate XIV
Rothschild's Lobe-billed Bird of Paradise. Hand-coloured lithograph by H. Grönvold from *Novitates Zoologicae* (1903), Pl.1.

LOCATION OF SPECIMENS

New York, two specimens.

H. Grönvold del. et. lith.

Mintern Bros. imp.

LOBORHAMPHUS NOBILIS Rothsch.

Rothschild's Lobe-Billed Bird of Paradise

Rothschild's Lobe-billed Bird of Paradise is known from just two specimens, one showing traces of immaturity, now in the collection of the American Museum of Natural History, New York.

Both birds once belonged to Walter Rothschild but they crossed the Atlantic in 1931 when the English lord sold up most of his vast collection of stuffed birds and cabinet skins. He had acquired his first Lobe-billed bird in 1901, through the agency of the Dutch merchant and bird of paradise specialist Renesse van Duivenbode. With no reason to suppose his bird represented anything other than a legitimate new species, Rothschild described it as *Loborhamphus nobilis*. His second lobe-billed came, several years later, via another Dutchman whose name, like Duivenbode's, has more than one association with the lost birds of paradise – J. Bensbach. Although both specimens have, therefore, something of a Dutch connection, there is little doubt that the Dutch simply traded them from New Guinea natives and that these natives were themselves probably not the plume hunters who had actually trapped them.

Neither bird arrived in Europe with any locality data more specific than the vast area then known as 'Dutch New Guinea'. Mary LeCroy (pers. comm.) of the American Museum of Natural History believes that neither came from the Arfak Mountains as the skins were not prepared in the manner used by Arfak natives, but this judgement,

Figure 16
Walter Rothschild's vast bird collection, packed and ready for dispatch to the American Museum of Natural History, New York. Courtesy of The Hon. Miriam Rothschild.

helpful though it is, rules out only a comparatively small area. The fact remains that the birds could have come from almost anywhere in the western half of New Guinea, and maybe from even further afield.

Rothschild's Lobe-bill is one of the most intriguing of all the lost birds of paradise. As with the others, a hybrid origin has been suggested and, since 1930 when Erwin Stresemann first proposed it, this interpretation of the two enigmatic skins has gained general acceptance. So many of Stresemann's diagnoses are demonstrably correct that the temptation to consider them all unchallengeable has proved a considerable one. Even when dealing with particularly cryptic forms his judgement as to parentage is usually full of insight. But Rothschild's Lobe-bill defies a solution. No really satisfactory conclusion can be arrived at from a study of the plumage evidence. The combination of features shown by *Loborhamphus nobilis* is too complex to unravel. Any two species selected at random from a dozen or so could be nominated as parental contenders, but each individual claim would be based on only the most tenuous or generalised of connections.

There are facial wattles that might be a link with one of several species. A metallic coloured edging to the pectoral plumes might indicate an association with the Twelve-wired Bird (*Seleucidis melanoleuca*) or with one of the four sicklebills (genus *Epimachus* or *Drepanornis*). A green band on the lower breast might suggest the Magnificent Rifle Bird (*Ptiloris magnificus*) or, when allied with the longish central tail feathers (these are, unfortunately, missing in one of the specimens), might indicate the interaction of *Astrapia*. Lengthened breast and neck feathers possibly betray the influence of the Superb Bird (*Lophorina superba*). The purple glitter on the breast might point to Queen Carola's Six-wired Bird (*Parotia carolae*). And so one could go on! Other features are quite original – a lovely violet cap that matches the glittering breast, for instance. Complicating the issue still further is the existence of a rather similar, but by no means identical, lost bird of paradise. This is Sharpe's Lobe-billed Rifle Bird, a form considered close enough to Rothschild's Lobe-bill to earn it a place in the same genus (*Loborhamphus*) during the years when both were thought of as legitimate species. Quite how these birds relate to one another – if at all – remains a mystery.

Confronted by these bewildering considerations, Erwin Stresemann selected the Long-tailed Paradigalla (*Paradigalla carunculata*) and the Superb Bird of Paradise (*Lophorina superba*) as parents for *nobilis*. This is no more than a guess. It may prove an inspired one, but in the light of present knowledge it is unsafe. In selecting birds of the genus *Paradigalla* as putative parents, Stresemann was obviously influenced by the bare flaps of skin on the face of *nobilis*. In these he doubtless saw a dim reflection of Paradigalla's heavy wattling. The issue of facial ornamentation may be a red herring, however. No less than four problematical birds of paradise and five legitimate species show some degree of wattling, and three further species show large areas of exposed facial skin.

On ethological grounds the pairing of Long-tailed Paradigalla and Superb Bird of Paradise seems unlikely. The Paradigalla is much bigger than the Superb. Sexes are virtually identical in *Paradigalla* but wildly different in the Superb – the male being highly ornamented and the female prettily, but soberly, striped. The Long-tailed Paradigalla's mating display is, apparently, unrecorded but, with its sexes so similar,

Plate XV
Superb Bird of Paradise (*Lophorina superba*) – males above and below right, female below left. Hand-coloured lithograph by J. Wolf and J. Smit from D.G. Elliot's *Monograph of the Paradiseidae* (London, 1873), Pl.9.

Plate XVI
The type specimen of *Loborhamphus nobilis* (undersides). Courtesy of the American Museum of Natural History.

PARADIGALLA CARUNCULATA

Plate XVII
Long-tailed Paradigalla (*Paradigalla carunculata*). Hand-coloured lithograph by J. Wolf and J. Smit from D.G. Elliot's *Monograph of the Paradiseidae* (London, 1873), Pl.17.

Plate XVIII
The type specimen of *Loborhamphus nobilis* (upper parts). Courtesy of the American Museum of Natural History

Figure 17
The bizarre climax to the highly
stylised display of the Superb Bird of
Paradise. The cape and breast plate
are used to produce a most
unbirdlike effect.

its display probably has few points of contact with the Superb Bird's highly stylised
ritual. With birds of paradise, however, one never knows.

Stresemann's masterpiece of ornithological detection might have balanced perfectly had he not pursued his brilliantly conceived general hypothesis to a positive
conclusion in each individual case. Sometimes the available evidence is not adequate
to allow a solution. In the instance of *Lorborhamphus nobilis* Stresemann's argument
gets little further than its starting points: other lost birds of paradise can be clearly
shown to be of mixed parentage; the home grounds of this particular bird have never
been found.

Until such time as more powerful evidence to the contrary is forthcoming, *Loborhamphus nobilis* can be regarded as a beautiful and quite 'proper' species. Whether it is now extinct or survives hidden in some forgotten or little known corner of New Guinea cannot, of course, be said.

THE ASTRAPIAN SICKLEBILL

Epimachus fastosus × *Astrapia nigra*

Epimachus astrapioides Rothschild, 1898, *Bulletin of the British Ornithologists' Club*, 7, p.22.
Falcinellus astrapioides Rothschild, 1898, *Das Tierreich – Aves*, lief 2, p.30.
Epimachus fastosus × *Astrapia nigra* Stresemann, 1930, *Novitates Zoologicae*, 36, p.13.
Astrapimachus astrapioides Mayr, 1941, *List of New Guinea Birds*, p.184.

DESCRIPTION

Head and upper neck brilliant metallic purple with bare post-ocular spot; back and rump brownish black with spangling of metallic green on back; tail black with steel blue and purple glossing; wings black; chin and throat blackish purple; lower throat metallic coppery red fading into coppery green on breast; abdomen green, base half of each feather black; flank plumes long – extending beyond wings – coloured green shading into coppery olive and mixed with fan-like feathers of purple edged with blue.

MEASUREMENTS

Length 830 mm (33 inches); wing 185 mm; tail 595 mm; bill 37 mm; tarsus 50 mm.

PLACE OF ORIGIN

Plate XIX
Astrapian Sicklebill.
Chromolithograph after a painting
by H. Grönvold from *Novitates
Zoologicae* (1911), Pl.7.

North-west New Guinea.

LOCATION OF SPECIMEN

New York.

Novitates Zoologicæ Vol. XVIII. 1911

Pl. VII

Repr.: A. Frisch, Berlin W

The Astrapian Sicklebill

In October of 1931, Walter Rothschild, beset by fears of a blackmail scandal and swamped by financial worries, sold his precious collection of bird skins to the American Museum of Natural History. The news came as a bombshell to the ornithological world when it was made public.

More than fifty years of unrelenting effort had resulted in the most important private collection of natural history objects that the world has yet seen. In his furious pursuit of the rare and the curious, Rothschild had financed whole expeditions to far-flung parts of the globe, sponsored agents to thoroughly scour markets and ports around the world, erected a purpose-built museum and hired experienced staff as curators. Day after day, week after week, year after year, parcels, packages and wooden crates filled with specimens of all kinds, arrived at Rothschild's headquarters in Tring, Hertfordshire. Dozens of explorers, field collectors, zoologists and agents would make the pilgrimage to the small country town some thirty miles north of London to unload their wares, request funds for their various ventures or simply to steep themselves in the atmosphere of enthusiasm that surrounded Rothschild and his thriving museum. Yet at the height of its completeness and influence the decision was taken to part with one of the museum's most important elements. One can only imagine the blackness of depression that drove poor Walter to part with those things he loved most.

Although he had interested himself in all branches of natural history, it was the birds that were his chief delight, and of the birds his favourites were the cassowaries, closely followed by the birds of paradise. Under no circumstances could Rothschild bear to part with his cassowaries (alive or stuffed) and vainly he struggled to have the birds of paradise also excluded from the sale. This was not to be, however, and his unbelievably fine collection crossed the ocean along with the rest. His librarian, a Miss Phyllis Thomas, supervised the transportation of the collection to New York, and Rothschild's niece Miriam (1983) described the circumstances of her home-coming:

> When she returned, Walter climbed the staircase to her office and asked for an account of the new installation. He listened intently – as usual in silence – but halfway through the narrative he was overcome with emotion and hurriedly left the room.

Among the vast array of birds that he had parted with were many great ornithological rarities; a very few treasures were unique. One of these unique types was a spectacular and very beautiful long-tailed bird of paradise that had come to Rothschild in 1898, purchased from Renesse van Duivenbode. As with other mysterious paradise birds, this particular one arrived in Europe without precise locality data, north-west New Guinea being the only information supplied. It has a head of purple, flank plumes of purple, blue and green, a tail of black glossed with blue and underparts sporting a combination of purple, green, and red. On receiving this remarkable creature Rothschild had, of course, immediately realised that it was not quite like anything that he'd seen before, but perhaps even he would be surprised to learn that a century later his specimen remains solitary.

One can imagine the delight with which Rothschild turned the specimen over and over in his hands causing the colours to glint in the light, and one can picture him poring over it for hours in his study, laying it lovingly alongside his incomparable series of other long-tailed paradise birds. In fact, Rothschild quickly became aware of his new bird's resemblance to two already well-known species, despite his being unable to match it exactly with either. These species are the Black Sicklebill (*Epimachus fastosus*) and the Arfak Astrapia (*Astrapia nigra*). Plumage characteristics of both were quite apparent in the feathers of the new bird so Rothschild, in his initial description of it, proposed the very appropriate name *Epimachus astrapioides* – the sicklebill like an astrapia – for what he supposed to be a new and legitimate species.

In most respects *astrapioides* is exactly intermediate between the Black Sicklebill and the Arfak Astrapia, and Erwin Stresemann proposed these as its parents when he reviewed all rare birds of paradise in 1930. Geographical and altitudinal ranges of these two species allow them to come into contact in the mountains of the Vogelkop – an area, incidentally, quite compatible with the vague locality data given for *astrapioides*. There seems little doubt that this glory of the old Tring Museum is a hybrid and, assuming its uniqueness to be significant, one that occurs only very infrequently.

Figure 18
Walter Rothschild seated between Albert Einstein (left) and George Bernard Shaw. Courtesy of The Hon. Miriam Rothschild.

ELLIOT'S BIRD OF PARADISE

Epimachus ellioti Ward, 1873

Epimachus ellioti Ward, 1873, *Proceedings of the Zoological Society*, p.742.

Falcinellus ellioti Rothschild, 1898, *Das Tierreich – Aves*, lief 2, p.29.

Pseudastrapia lobata Rothschild, 1907, *Bulletin of the British Ornithologists' Club*, 21, p.25.

Pseudastrapia ellioti Rothschild, 1911, *Ibis*, p.361.

Epimachus fastosus × *Astrapia nigra* Stresemann, 1930, *Novitates Zoologicae*, 36, p.13.

Epimachus fastosus × *Paradigalla carunculata* Stresemann, 1930, *Novitates Zoologicae, 36, p.13.*

Astrapimachus ellioti Mayr, 1941, *List of New Guinea Birds*, p.184.

DESCRIPTION

Adult (ellioti): general colour dark, almost black, with much violet iridescence; forehead black giving way to metallic violet crown; chin, nape and sides of head black with olive green sheen on cheeks; back blackish with gloss of metallic violet; throat velvet blackish brown merging into wash of olive green on upper breast followed, lower down, by broad band of faded red grape shading again into an olive green wash extending to flank plumes; pectoral shields tipped with crescents of metallic purplish blue (second set more narrowly than first); wings blackish brown illuminated with violet gloss appearing grape green in some lights; tail black richly sheened with violet; bill black, long, thin and downcurved with orange yellow lobing at gape.

Immature (lobata): generally dullish with forehead bottle green and central retrices showing blue glossing; bill and feet black.

MEASUREMENTS

Length 540–550 mm (21 inches); wing 188–202 mm; tail 395–405 mm; bill 42–50 mm; tarsus 46–50 mm.

PLACE OF ORIGIN

North-west New Guinea.

LOCATION OF SPECIMENS

Adult (ellioti): Dresden, London (Tring). *Immature (lobata)*: New York.

Plate XX
Elliot's Bird of Paradise. Hand-coloured lithograph by J. Gould and W. Hart from J. Gould's *Birds of New Guinea* (London, 1875–88), Pl.8.

Elliot's Bird of Paradise

During the month of September, 1873, a London taxidermist, Edwin Ward, received, among a collection of freshly imported skins, an example of a very beautiful yet hitherto unknown sickle-billed bird of paradise. Recognising immediately the unique nature of his possession, Ward described and exhibited it – imperfect in that it lacked feet and primary feathers – before The Zoological Society of London. At this meeting he proposed the name *Epimachus ellioti* in honour of the American author, D.G. Elliot, whose lavish work on birds of paradise was shortly to be available. For comparative purposes, Ward had taken with him two examples of the already familiar Black Sicklebill (*Epimachus fastosus*) and he pointed out significant differences. The new bird was one third less in size. Instead of being bluish green on the back and tail it was 'beautifully illuminated with an amethyst colour'. The plumage was thicker and noticeably more velvety in texture and the breast was greenish with a line on the chest of 'indefinite tertiary shades'. The back lacked the spangling that occurs on the Black Sicklebill, but an additional, and surprising, feature was a skin flap attached to the gape. Being a native trade skin there was no locality data for the bird and little else for Ward to say. He concluded his description with remarks relating to parasites:

> I beg leave to exhibit a curious parasite taken from the breast of Elliot's *Epimachus*. In form this creature more resembles a sheep tick than a bird louse. I have before now seen similar parasites, especially on *E. magnus* [*E. fastosus*]. I believe the parasites of birds of paradise remain as yet undescribed.

Within three months, Ward's bird – presumably de-loused – had been drawn by the great wildlife artist Joseph Wolf, and the resulting illustration was included in Elliot's *Monograph of the Paradiseidae* (1873). This particular picture (see Frontispiece) is certainly very beautiful but is quite misleading in the impression it gives of the bird's appearance. Much closer to reality is the illustration (*see* p. 55) – for which the same specimen served as model – given in John Gould's partly posthumous publication *The Birds of New Guinea* (1875–88). This plate was used again a few years afterwards by Richard Bowdler Sharpe for his *Monograph of the Paradiseidae* (1891–98), and Wolf's plate was shamelessly copied for C.B. Cory's *Beautiful and Curious Birds of the World* (1883). Thus, portraits of a single trade skin grace the pages of four of the nineteenth century's most lavish bird books.

The bird itself passed quite quickly to John Gould who, in addition to being well-known for his magnificent ornithological tomes, was celebrated for his tenacity in prising rare specimens from the cabinets of rivals and adding them to his own. Much of his extensive collection was eventually sold privately, but what remained at his death in 1881 was sent to the British Museum and this included the type specimen of *Epimachus ellioti*. The handwritten listing relating to it can be seen in the ornithological accessions register kept at the Museum's sub-department of ornithology at Tring. On p.93 of the volume covering the years 1880–1884 is the following entry: 1881.5.1.1696/*Epimachus ellioti*/Waigiou?/Type of species.

At the time of my first interest in this bird, Mr I.C.J. Galbraith (then of the BMNH)

was unable to locate the skin, and although he and I searched the collection of type specimens and the collection of birds of paradise we had no success in finding it. Skins with adjacent numbers remained in place but of *ellioti* there was no sign. In a paper published in the *Bulletin of the British Ornithologists' Club* (1979), I described the specimen as lost. This had the fortunate result of stimulating Ian Galbraith's colleague Michael Walters into making a further search and, eventually, a re-discovery. Due to its controversial nature, *ellioti* had, years previously, been put aside for study and then forgotten.

This highly important skin is not unique, however, for in 1890 A.B. Meyer, then Director of the Dresden Museum, received another example – this one from the Dutch merchants Duivenbode, the father and son team who were often in the habit of sending unusual birds to noted ornithologists of the day. Herr S. Eck of the Staaliches Museum für Tierkunde has confirmed the continuing existence of item C9933 (despite the obliteration of old Dresden by Allied bombing during World War II) and supplied photographs. It is a perfect male obtained, like the type, without proper locality data, the place of origin being recorded as north-west New Guinea.

A specimen, possibly additional to the two already mentioned, was known to Richard Bowdler Sharpe who remarked on it thus:

Figure 19
(Above, left), The celebrated nineteenth-century wildlife artist Joseph Wolf (1820–99).

Figure 20
(Above, right), Adolf Bernhard Meyer (1840–1911), Director of the Dresden Museum and describer of several new birds of paradise. Courtesy of the Staatliches Museum für Tierkunde, Dresden.

I have seen a perfect skin of *E. ellioti* which was offered by a dealer to the British Museum, but the price demanded was so exorbitant that I was not able to recommend the purchase of the specimen and I do not know what has become of it.

Ernst Hartert (1919), who looked after the bird section of Walter Rothschild's museum, believed this to be the bird acquired by Dresden. This is probably the case but, if so, it is surprising to find that Sharpe was unfamiliar with the details. No additional adult specimens are recorded but, almost certainly, an immature example exists at the American Museum of Natural History. This remarkable skin was one of Rothschild's acquisitions and came to him in 1907, having been imported to Europe by J. Bensbach, one-time Dutch resident at Ternate. Predictably, the locality data is extremely vague – Dutch New Guinea!

In line with his regular custom concerning unusual birds, Rothschild lost no time in firing off a description for publication in the *Bulletin of the British Ornithologists' Club*, proposing the name *Pseudastrapia lobata* for his new 'species'. It is perhaps not being too unkind to Rothschild to suggest that zeal for the discovery of new species may have caused him to overlook or disregard the probability of his *lobata* being an immature *ellioti*. Hartert (1919), his own curator, thought that it was, but no later researcher (including Stresemann) appears to have examined the possibility in any depth.

The case for the proposition can be made out quite clearly. *Pseudastrapia lobata* is blackish in colour, the only iridescence being a violet tinge along the shafts of the two central tail feathers – just what might be expected in the immature of *ellioti*. Measurements are compatible (length 540 mm *lobata*, 550 mm *ellioti*, tail 395 mm *lobata*, 405 mm *ellioti*; tarsus 46 mm *lobata* 50 mm *ellioti*) although bill lengths cannot be properly compared as the young bird's beak is broken near its tip (*lobata* 42 mm, *ellioti* 50 mm). Even more telling is the distinctive lobing of the gape that is present in both forms, and also a peculiar structure of the tail that the birds share: the two long, central tail feathers are pointed whereas the shorter ones have blunter, barbed ends.

Due to their extreme rarity *ellioti* and *lobata* were included in Stresemann's (1930) review of lost birds of paradise. Each was, however, considered separately. For *ellioti*, Stresemann proposed the Black Sicklebill (*Epimachus fastosus*) and the Arfak Astrapia (*Astrapia nigra*) as parents, founding his hypothesis on plumage characteristics he held to be significant. Examination of the type specimen of *ellioti*, however, gives little reason to suppose it anything other than unmixed *Epimachus*. This, in itself, may not mean that hybrid origin can be eliminated from the range of possibilities (a hybrid may, of course, resemble just one of its parents) but neither does it provide a basis for any such belief.

A connection with *Epimachus* being apparent, it may be said that the bird appears much as one might expect an unknown species of sicklebill to appear. The grounds given by Stresemann for associating it with *Astrapia* are, therefore, crucial. These he cites as an indication of red and green on the underparts and an alleged similarity of the tails. Taken at face value this may or may not be considered conclusive, but when critically examined the connections are tenuous. The belly and lower breast is certainly green but this is in the nature of a wash and not reminiscent of the iridescent shield of the Arfak Astrapia; it might be added that green is not a particularly unusual colour

in tropical birds. The faded red, shading broadly across these green underparts, is similarly quite unlike the vivid, narrow, metallic red band on the breast of the putative parent. The tail feathers of *ellioti* resemble those of *nigra* only in the iridescent violet of their upper surface, but the significance of this is unclear for the tail of the other alleged parent; the Black Sicklebill, generally having a bluer sheen, will also show a violet hue in some lights.

The alleged hybrid is considerably smaller than either supposed parent and, likewise, sports a tail shorter then either. Both 'parents' lack two of *ellioti*'s most distinctive features – the unmistakable lobing of the gape and a peculiar barbed shaping to the tips of the shorter tail feathers, an arrangement resembling that shown by the Long-tailed Paradigalla (*Paradigalla carunculata*). Stresemann was clearly perplexed by the gape lobing (although he makes no mention of the shape of the tail) and in rather cavalier fashion he concluded his analysis with a passing suggestion that the interaction of *Paradigalla* (a genus that, in addition to the similarity of the tail feathers, also

Plate XXI
The Ruling Passion (sometimes called *The Ornithologist*). Oil painting by Sir John Everett Millais (1829–96). This celebrated Victorian painting is thought to have been inspired by a visit the artist paid to the house of John Gould shortly before the latter's death. An old collector – perhaps too ill to rise – is shown inspecting his prize possessions, some of them birds of paradise, brought to his couch by devoted members of his family.

carries facial wattles) would account for this. This is hardly acceptable. It cannot be stated that one bird is the hybrid of two others while mentioning a fourth to account for certain conspicuous characters. Yet in order to make his already stretched hypothesis preferable to a tentative recognition of *ellioti* as a species, even more refinement was required. Stresemann had used the combination of Black Sicklebill and Arfak Astrapia to account (almost certainly correctly) for a distinctly different problematical form – the bird described as *Epimachus astrapioides*, the Astrapian Sicklebill. To explain this doubling up he suggested that the one kind represented the reciprocal cross of the other (i.e. male sicklebill × female astrapia as opposed to female sicklebill × male astrapia). There may be nothing intrinsically wrong with this idea, but neither is there direct evidence in support. It could equally well be said that a different sicklebill or a different astrapia (*splendidissima*, for instance) is involved for there is no locality data to tie *ellioti* (or *astrapioides*) to the Arfak Mountains, the only known home of the Arfak Astrapia.

For the probable immature of *ellioti*, Rothschild's *Pseudastrapia lobata*, Stresemann was forced to choose different putative parents, a necessary course of action if the two forms are regarded as distinct and both options of the reciprocal cross have been taken up. Also, Stresemann may have believed (although he does not say so) that *lobata* did not come from the Arfak Mountains (Mary LeCroy, of the American Museum of Natural History, assures me that its manner of preparation excludes this possibility), an idea that necessarily eliminates the Arfak Astrapia as a potential parent.

The gape lobing on the face of *ellioti* had puzzled Stresemann, but its presence on *ellioti*'s congener *lobata* gave him an opportunity to pigeon-hole it. He therefore retained the Black Sicklebill as a parent for *lobata* and introduced the Long-tailed Paradigalla, complete with facial wattles, as the other. There may or may not be a connection between the pronounced wattling of *Paradigalla* and the mere flap of skin carried by *lobata*, but if the flap is such a significant feature, why then should it be disregarded in the case of *ellioti*? Presumably, Stresemann wished to exclude *Paradigalla* from *ellioti*'s parentage because of its black underparts, a colouring that leaves the green and red of the alleged hybrid unexplained. Yet *Paradigalla*, with its peculiar tail feather structure, its wattling and its smaller size, makes a rather better parent for *ellioti* than Stresemann's proposition *Astrapia nigra*. With the additional advantage that it does not necessarily tie *ellioti* to the Arfak Mountains, *Paradigalla carunculata* × *Epimachus fastosus* can certainly be regarded as a serious possibility for the origin of this mysterious bird. If *ellioti* is actually a hybrid, then these two species are almost certainly its parents.

Stresemann's unstated argument against the legitimacy of both *ellioti* and *lobata* can be put simply: since many problematic birds of paradise *are* demonstrably hybrids, *all* must therefore be so, and suitable parents may be selected accordingly. The unsatisfactory nature of this did not quite escape Walter Rothschild who added some notes of his own to Stresemann's article, but these, unfortunately, only cloud the issue still further. In his notes he expressed general agreement with points raised, but dissatisfaction with the designation for *ellioti*. Rothschild's contribution to the study of birds in general, and the Paradiseidae in particular, was enormous, but in this case his opinions were fanciful:

The possibility exists that it is a tri-generic hybrid. I prefer to consider
Pseudastrapia [*Epimachus*] *ellioti* as a secondary hybrid of either *Pseudastrapia lobata*
× *Astrapia nigra* or of *Epimachus astrapioides* × *Paradigalla carunculata*. But . . . it
appears better to leave this an open question.

Figures 21–23
Three views of the Dresden
specimen of Elliot's Bird of Paradise.
Courtesy of the Staatliches Museum
für Tierkunde, Dresden.

This would make *ellioti* a secondary hybrid involving initial hybrids that are known by
only half as many specimens as their own progeny, and assumes fertility retention
between no less than three genera.

ASTRAPIA NIGRA.

Plate XXII
Arfak Astrapia (*Astrapia nigra*) –
males top and centre, female below.
Hand-coloured lithograph by J.
Gould and W. Hart from J. Gould's
Birds of New Guinea (London,
1875–88), Pl.17.

EPIMACHUS SPECIOSUS, (Bodd.)

Plate XXIII
Black Sicklebill (*Epimachus fastosus*) –
males top and bottom, female
centre. Hand-coloured lithograph
from R. Bowdler Sharpe's *Monograph
of the Paradiseidae* (London, 1891–8),
Pl.14.

Perhaps the most extraordinary feature of the case of Elliot's Bird of Paradise is the fact that all these arguments have remained virtually unchallenged. Sometimes the work of later ornithologists has served only to add to the confusion. Ernst Mayr, for instance, Stresemann's pupil and a stickler for correctness in matters of nomenclature and scientific rigour, lapsed curiously when compiling his *List of New Guinea Birds* (1941). He provided a new genus name, *Astrapimachus*, for *ellioti* and *astrapioides*, both forms that he considered hybrids and therefore invalid as species. There is little doubt that it was the influence of this kind of sloppiness that led to the British Museum's invaluable example being removed from the carefully curated collection of type specimens and misplaced with birds of less certain value.

Elliot's Bird of Paradise may indeed be a hybrid (*Paradigalla carunculata* × *Epimachus fastosus* being by far the most likely combination) but it is equally likely that this is a species in its own right, referable – as originally believed – to the genus *Epimachus*. The early workers – Ward, Elliot, Gould, Sharpe and Meyer – who handled specimens when comparatively fresh, saw no reason to doubt it.

There was at one time some speculation over where such a bird might be found. The lack of feet and primary feathers led to a supposition that the type had come from Waigeu, an island off the north-western end of New Guinea where this kind of preparation was regularly used. The idea held certain attractions, for although neither the Black Sicklebill nor the closely related Brown (*Epimachus meyeri*) are known to occur on Waigeu, there is some evidence that a sicklebill lives, or did once live, on the island. The eighteenth-century French explorer Labillardière claimed to have acquired one there:

> I killed a great many fierce birds, among others the species of *Promerops* [Sicklebill] which Buffon calls the *Promerops* of New Guinea.

Whether or not the example was taken back to France is not made clear in Labillardière's book, *Voyage in Search of La Perouse*, and no precise identification can be made from the author's vague description. Much later, the Italian collector Odoardo Beccari heard, although was never able to substantiate, that an *Epimachus* was indeed to be found on Waigeu. Even assuming these reports to be based on fact, there would still be no solid ground for supposing that the bird in question is, or was, *ellioti*, but such a suggestion is, naturally, tantalising.

If Elliot's Bird of Paradise actually constitutes a species, and if it still exists, it must be either exceedingly rare or, perhaps more likely, very localised. It would most probably be a species of high altitudes (the Black Sicklebill frequents heights up to 8,000 feet – 2,500 metres – and the Brown can occur above 9,250 feet – 3,000 metres) and, as many high-altitude areas were never regularly visited by plume hunters, this might have some bearing on the extreme rarity of specimens. Jared Diamond (1972) has pointed out that the avifaunas supported by different mountains just a few miles apart, are by no means necessarily identical, and it is well-known that a number of New Guinea bird species have distributions that are very patchy. Although perhaps common at certain select, but scattered, localities, a species may be altogether absent in other seemingly suitable habitats. Alternatively, it is quite possible that Elliot's Bird of Paradise is now extinct, having failed to withstand competition from one of its close relatives.

The comparatively recent (January 1981) re-discovery of a gardener bower bird, the Yellow-fronted (*Amblyornis flavifrons*) – previously known, like *Epimachus ellioti*, only from trade skins – provides at least some hope that this lovely creature may one day be found in some overlooked corner or mountain fastness of New Guinea. And if the bird proves, after all, to be a hybrid, then it will be no less beautiful for that.

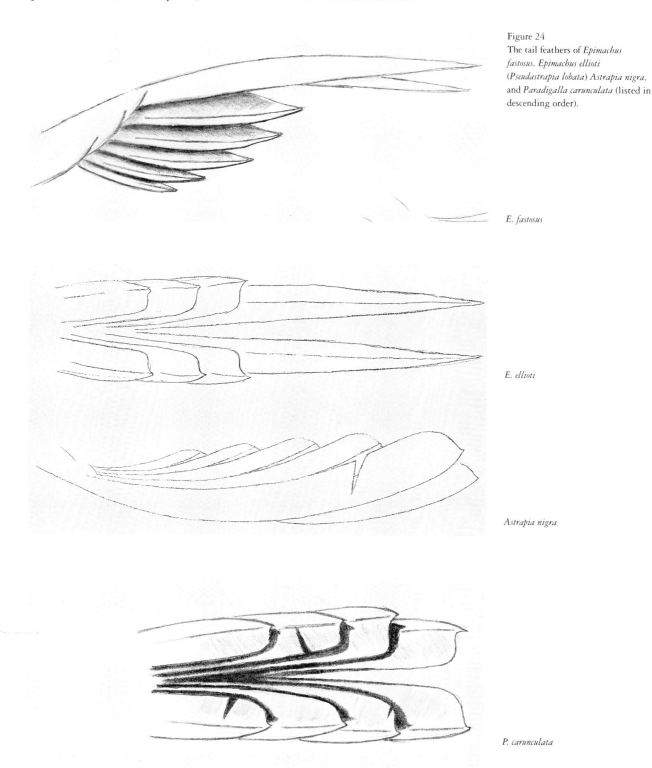

Figure 24
The tail feathers of *Epimachus fastosus, Epimachus ellioti* (*Pseudastrapia lobata*) *Astrapia nigra,* and *Paradigalla carunculata* (listed in descending order).

E. fastosus

E. ellioti

Astrapia nigra

P. carunculata

THE MYSTERIOUS BIRD OF BOBAIRO

Epimachus fastosus × *Lophorina superba?*

Epimachus fastosus atratus × *Lophorina superba feminina* Junge, 1953, Zoological Results of the Dutch New Guinea Expedition, 1939. *Zoologische Verhandelingen, Leiden*, 20, p.62.

DESCRIPTION
Crown metallic greenish blue; rest of head black; mantle black with purplish gloss; some elongated black feathers on sides of neck and a series of axe-shaped, blue-tipped feathers on flanks; rest of upper parts black; throat and breast black richly suffused with purplish blue; rest of underparts black; tail absent in only known specimen; iris chocolate brown; bill grey; feet grey.

MEASUREMENTS
Length (without tail) 250 mm (10 inches); wing 168 mm; bill 43 mm; tarsus 41 mm.

PLACE OF ORIGIN
Bobairo, Wissel Lakes, Irian Jaya.

Plate XXIV
The Mysterious Bird of Bobairo. Oil
painting by Mary Philcox.

LOCATION OF SPECIMEN
Leiden.

The Mysterious Bird of Bobairo

On 14 September 1939, just as war was breaking out in Europe, a Dutch collecting expedition to the Wissel Lakes area of south-western New Guinea encountered a very peculiar bird. The expedition had stopped at Bobairo, near Enarotali on the shores of Lake Paniai, and here a bird was collected that, with its axe-shaped, blue-tipped pectoral feathers, resembled, at first sight, a Black Sicklebill (*Epimachus fastosus*). However, the most characteristic feature of the Sicklebill – the long, slender, down-curved beak – was present only in a much modified form. The bill of this Bobairo bird was considerably shorter and more stubby and showed no greater tendency to down-curve than that of many other bird of paradise species. Nor was the beak the only sicklebill feature that was missing. The glittering spangling of the back and the long black pectoral plumes were wanting, and although the Bobairo bird lacked these characteristics, it introduced others that were quite new. A purplish blue gloss suffused the feathers of the throat and breast and some longish black feathers extended from the sides of the neck. Unfortunately, the bird's tail was missing so there is no way of knowing how it might have compared with that of other species; as the Black Sicklebill has an extraordinarily long tail, a comparison might have been particularly revealing.

Due to the disruption caused by World War II, it was not until 1953 that a written report on the expedition's findings was published. By this time the specimens themselves had arrived in Holland and been deposited in the Leiden Museum, an institution that houses one of the world's most important scientific collections of birds.

G.C.A. Junge painstakingly worked through and described the specimens that had been collected more than a decade earlier, including the unique find from the shores of Lake Paniai. Influenced, presumably, by the apparent tendency of the Paradiseidae to hybridise and reluctant, therefore, to describe a new species on the basis of a single anomalous skin – Junge decided that the bird was probably a hybrid. He thought it most likely resulted from the crossing of the Black Sicklebill with the Superb Bird of Paradise (*Lophorina superba*), surprising though such a cross might seem. Junge considered the Magnificent Rifle Bird (*Ptiloris magnificus*) as a substitute for the Superb Bird but finally rejected the idea as it left the elongated black feathers at the sides of the neck unexplained. Also, the beak and the length of wing and tarsus are intermediate between *Epimachus* and *Lophorina* yet smaller than might be expected in a cross between sicklebill and rifle bird. Against this it might be said that hybridisation between this latter pair is rather easier to envisage than a crossing between the Superb Bird and a very much larger sicklebill.

The Mysterious Bird of Bobairo remains unique and its true status is still uncertain. Even its actual appearance in life can only be guessed at because of the absence of a tail in the only known specimen; if it does, as is supposed, have a connection with the Black Sicklebill then the tail might be very spectacular. The bird may, of course, not be a hybrid at all, but, if it is, Junge's carefully considered analysis probably reflects the truth.

Figure 25
Map showing the location of Bobairo on the shores of Lake Paniai, Wissel Lakes, Irian Jaya.

LAKE PANIAI

Bobairo

Enarotali

Figure 26
The Europeans (from the left: F.J.
Wissel, J. Dozy and Dr de Hartog)
who discovered the Wissel Lakes,
with some of the people they found
there.

BARNES' ASTRAPIA

Astrapia mayeri × *Astrapia stephaniae*

Astrarchia barnesi Iredale, 1948, *Australian Zoologist*, 2, p.160.
Astrapia mayeri × *Astrapia stephaniae* Sims, 1956, *Bulletin of the British Museum (Natural History), Zoology*, 3, p.425.

DESCRIPTION

A variable hybrid showing differing degrees of the influence of its parents *Astrapia mayeri* and *Astrapia stephaniae*.

Most intermediate form: forehead iridescent green with slight tuft above bill; crown greenish blue; rest of face and large bib on throat iridescent green; back and wings blackish brown; breast band (below green bib) velvety black bordered below with narrow band of coppery red; rest of underparts blackish brown; tail long and black, narrowing towards base and showing large area coloured white; iris dark brown; bill and feet black.

MEASUREMENTS

Length 840 mm (33 inches); wing 170 mm; tail 700 mm; bill 18 mm; tarsus 44 mm.

PLACE OF ORIGIN

Mount Hagen.

LOCATION OF SPECIMENS

London (Tring), Sydney.

Plate XXV
Barnes' Astrapia. Oil Painting by
Errol Fuller.

Barnes' Astrapia

Figure 27
Fred Shaw Mayer.

Near the end of 1938 two very long, white tail feathers with black tips were sent to the British Museum from New Guinea. The sender was Fred Shaw Mayer, a long-time resident and explorer of the land. Following up rumours that an unknown bird of paradise existed in the wild country to the west of Mount Hagen, Shaw Mayer had set off in search of the truth. In terms of finding the birds themselves his journey was a failure, but his return wasn't completely empty-handed. In a letter to the British Museum he wrote:

> In the middle of last August I was given by a missionary the two tail feathers I am sending you. They were taken out of the hair on the head of a Mount Hagen native . . . I give the feathers to the Museum quite freely.

The feathers themselves and the circumstantial evidence supplied by Shaw Mayer were enough to convince C.R. Stonor, of the British Museum, that a new species did,

Figure 28
Papuan tribesmen in head-dresses made from the feathers and plumes of birds of paradise.

Figure 29
(Left), Otto Finsch (1838–1917).

Figure 30
(Right), Crown Prince Rudolph of Austria and Princess Stephanie (circa 1885).

in fact, exist. Appropriately, he named it *Astrapia mayeri* after the gentleman who had been so generous with his find. When, soon afterwards, complete specimens of the bird became available, Stonor's diagnosis was found to be remarkably accurate. Not only was the bird new to science, its placement in the genus *Astrapia* was absolutely correct. Thus, Shaw Mayer's Bird of Paradise (or the Ribbon-tailed, as it is now more usually called) came to the attention of naturalists, and it remains the most recently discovered bird of paradise species.

Its close relative *Astrapia stephaniae* has been known for considerably longer. In 1884, the explorer Karl Hunstein plunged into cannibal-infested jungle and emerged not just with his life but with no less than three new bird of paradise species – a splendid sicklebill, the outrageously beautiful Prince Rudolph's Bird of Paradise, and a new astrapia. At Cooktown in Queensland he met, apparently by chance, the German naturalist Otto Finsch who had just 'annexed' no less a prize than 'Kaiser Wilhelm's Land' (a vast area of north-east New Guinea) for Germany. Already – presumably – basking in triumph, Finsch's additional delight when Hunstein offered to sell his ornithological treasures can easily be imaged. Hunstein, incidentally, was to push his luck once too often and drowned while attempting to reach New Britain in search of yet more new birds of paradise.

Finsch returned to Europe and set about naming his birds. The Sicklebill became *Epimachus meyeri* after his colleague A.B. Meyer; Hunstein had only obtained a female and with the full glory of the species remaining unknown, Finsch presumably felt able to allow himself this small indulgence. Different tactics were adopted for the two seemingly more impressive finds.

A custom of the day was to curry favour with the crowned heads of Europe by bestowing their royal names on new and beautiful creatures; several birds of paradise came by their names following this principle (although the naming of one, *Diphyllodes respublica*, was a defiant reaction to the trend). Otto Finsch, a poor man despite his scientific and political achievements, was sharply aware of the advantages of royal favour and chose to honour the House of Hapsburg with the two spectacular birds that remained unnamed. His beautiful blue bird he called *Paradisea rudolphi* after Crown Prince Rudolph of Austria and the lovely new long-tailed bird he named *Astrapia stephaniae* after Rudolph's wife, the Princess Stephanie. It cannot, alas, be recorded

Plate XXVI
Princess Stephanie's Bird of Paradise
(*Astrapia stephaniae*) – male front,
female behind. Hand-coloured
lithograph by W. Hart from R.
Bowdler Sharpe's *Monograph of the
Paradiseidae* (London, 1891–8),
Pl. 19.

that this incomparably flamboyant piece of flattery brought lasting happiness to the illustrious young couple. Their marriage ended five years later, at Mayerling, when Prince Rudolph died – together with his lover – from gunshot wounds, in what was, apparently, a suicide pact. The widowed Stephanie faded in importance and is now hardly remembered at all, but her bird of paradise is, perhaps, the best known of the five long-tailed species that make up the genus *Astrapia*. It is a reasonably common bird in the central mountains of eastern New Guinea, and at the western extremity (the Mount Hagen area) of its range comes into contact with its ribbon-tailed relative, *Astrapia mayeri*.

The two species are known to encounter one another in altitudinal zones of overlap on Mount Hagen itself, where they interbreed quite freely. Heights occupied by each species vary greatly from area to area, but Princess Stephanie's Bird generally takes the lower ground, between 4,800 (1,500 metres) and 9,000 feet (2,800 metres) with the Ribbon-tailed occupying altitudes from 5,800 (1,800 metres) to 11,000 feet (3,400 metres). Where they occur together, they tend to meet between 7,800 (2,400 metres) and 8,450 feet (2,600 metres) and it is at these heights that hybrids can be found. There is, apparently, a certain amount of gradation as the two species mix and museum examples show various stages of this process. At the lower elevations birds tend to be *Astrapia stephaniae* or hybrids closest to it, and at the higher ones the reverse is the case with the influence of *Astrapia mayeri* being more striking.

Plate XXVII
Ribbon-tailed Bird of Paradise (*Astrapia mayeri*). Oil painting by Errol Fuller.

Figure 31
Colonial days in German New
Guinea. An expatriate photographed
in the tub, circa 1915.

The hybrid form first came to attention when Captain Ned Blood procured a specimen during his war-time patrols in the Mount Hagen district. This beautiful bird
has the broad tail of Princess Stephanie's Bird but much of it is coloured white like
that of the Ribbon-tailed. It was inspected by Tom Iredale at the Australian Museum,
Sydney (where Captain Blood sent much of his material), who, not recognising the
hybrid origin, described it as a new species, *Astrarchia barnesi* in 1948. Soon after this,
however, Fred Shaw Mayer, finishing off the process he had started, discovered an
actual hybrid zone at Yanka, a zone that has subsequently been investigated by a
number of ornithologists.

The westward limits of the range of the Ribbon-tailed Bird of Paradise have not
been precisely determined. It is possible, perhaps even likely, that the Ribbon-tailed
comes into contact with another closely related species, the Splendid Astrapia
(*Astrapia splendidissima*). Several writers have speculated on the lovely form that might
result if these two species do actually meet!

Figure 32
(Left), Brown Sicklebill (*Epimachus meyeri*) – male below, female above. Hand-coloured lithograph by W. Hart from R. Bowdler Sharpe's *Monograph of the Paradiseidae* (London, 1891–8).

Figure 33
(Right), Splendid Astrapia (*Astrapia splendidissima*) – male above, female below. Hand-coloured lithograph by J.G. Keulemans from R. Bowdler Sharpe's *Monograph of the Paradiseidae* (London, 1891–8).

DUIVENBODE'S SIX-WIRED BIRD OF PARADISE

Lophorina superba × *Parotia sefilata*

Parotia duivenbodei Rothschild, 1900, *Bulletin of the British Ornithologists' Club*, 10, p.100.

Lophorina superba × *Parotia sefilata* Stresemann, 1930, *Novitates Zoologicae*, 36, p.12.

DESCRIPTION

Head black glossed deep purple with puff of feathers over bill (but these not elongated as in other *Parotias*) and wedge-shaped occipital patch of metallic bluish green; rest of upper parts black glossed purple; tail black glossed purple, feathers rather rounded at ends; large breast shield metallic green with feathers towards shield's edge showing blue borders; loose black feathers on flanks; abdomen blackish.

MEASUREMENTS

Length 280 mm (11 inches); wing 150 mm; tail 115 mm; bill 34 mm; tarsus 38 mm.

PLACE OF ORIGIN

Inland from Yaour (Jaur), Geelvink Bay.

LOCATION OF SPECIMENS

New York, Paris.

Plate XXVIII
Duivenbode's Six-wired Bird of
Paradise. Hand-coloured lithograph
by H. Grönvold from the *Ibis*
(1911), Pl.5.

Ibis.1911. Pl. V.

H.Grönvold del.et lith.

West,Newman imp.

PAROTIA DUIVENBODEI ♂.

Duivenbode's Six-Wired Bird of Paradise

During the last years of the nineteenth century and the first decades of the twentieth, the Dutch merchants van Duivenbode, originally a father and son team, operated out of the Moluccan port of Ternate. This port, large and influential by the standards of the region and situated on a small island of the same name, lies just to the west of the much bigger island of Halmahera. Some two hundred miles to the east, across the Halmahera Sea, is the western extremity of what was once Dutch New Guinea (now Irian Jaya). Most goods coming from this Dutch end of the great island would, of necessity, have passed through Ternate on the long journey to Europe, Asia or North America. The merchants van Duivenbode were, then, strategically placed to sift through the treasures that regularly arrived from the vast, virtually unknown land to their east.

Presumably they profited on a variety of trading fronts; certainly if their success in obtaining unusual bird skins can be used as a yardstick, their business must have thrived. Quite apart from acquiring many rare items on behalf of important museums

Figure 34
A Papuan hunter photographed just before World War I, when the Duivenbodes were making the last of their discoveries.

Figure 35
A nineteenth-century engraving
from *Cassell's Book of Birds* (London,
1889) showing a six-wired bird of
paradise with a lesser bird of
paradise (above) and a king bird
(below).

(Dresden, Paris and Tring among them), at least four of the lost birds of paradise first came to attention directly as a result of their efforts, and three of these were given the Duivenbode name: a 'rifle bird' (*Paryphephorus duivenbodei*), a 'plume bird' (*Paradisea duivenbodei*), and the aberrant six-wired bird known as *Parotia duivenbodei*. The Duivenbodes' pleasure in the attachment of their family name to these birds was probably considerable, and it seems rather a shame that each name was to become scientifically redundant when, in 1930, Erwin Stresemann struck them, one by one, from the list of legitimate species.

Paradise birds with six-head wires, each wire tipped at its end with a distinctive 'flag', had been known in Europe since quite early times. By the close of the nineteenth century, four species were recognised – all placed in the genus *Parotia* – and in the first year of the new century Walter Rothschild described, what then seemed, a fifth from a specimen sent him by the younger Duivenbode, Renesse. This bird had been purchased by Duivenbode from native hunters and, apart from the vague piece of information that it came from Dutch New Guinea, it arrived in Europe without locality data. Perceiving an affinity with the six-wired birds, Rothschild named it *Parotia duivenbodei*, but despite placing the new form in this genus he recognised certain obscure features: the breast shield he noted to be of unusual size and structure; the feathers were smaller than might be expected in a six-wired bird and compressed into a large number of rows; the metallic band at the back of the head, so characteristic of the genus, was, unaccountably, wedge-shaped – and, atypically, there was no trace of any white on the head.

Rothschild's bird, incidentally, possessed only two head wires, but this circumstance is not necessarily of significance as wear and accident can easily account for wire loss. When a second specimen was identified some years after the first, *all* the head wires were wanting. This second bird was, in fact, yet another Duivenbode discovery, with the Muséum d'Histoire Naturelle in Paris this time benefiting from their enterprise. Unlike many lost bird of paradise specimens, there was some locality data for this particular bird. It is alleged that it was taken inland from Yaour, Geelvink Bay (probably what is now called Waar Island).

With only two specimens known, Erwin Stresemann reviewed the form in his 1930 analysis of rare birds of paradise. Expecting to find a hybrid origin, he suggested the Superb Bird of Paradise (*Lophorina superba*) and the Arfak Six-wired Bird (*Parotia sefilata*) as parents. In many respects the ambiguous nature of *duivenbodei's* plumage supports the diagnosis and, certainly, opportunities for interbreeding would be considerable, the species inhabiting much common territory in the mountains of the Vogelkop. The idea of them combining is not one that is difficult to come to terms with, for these are closely related birds; Diamond (1972) even went so far as to lump *Parotia* into the genus *Lophorina*. Nor, ethologically, does there seem any great barrier to the occasional production of hybrids. Females of the Superb Bird look quite similar (remarkably so in some instances) to females of six-wired species. Superbs are known to be attracted to the 'courts' of six-wired birds, and similarities in the call notes and stepping dances of the two species have been noticed.

More surprising, perhaps, than the fact of hybridisation is the rarity of encounters with these hybrids. Probably this tells more about the formidable nature of New Guinea than about the actual incidence of any promiscuous activity. If, as surmised,

Plate XXIX
Arfak Six-wired Bird of Paradise (*Parotia sefilata*) – males in foreground, female in distance. Hand-coloured lithograph by J. Gould and W. Hart from J. Gould's *Birds of New Guinea* (London, 1875–88), Pl.25.

PAROTIA SEXPENNIS,

the Superb Bird crosses with one six-wired species, there seems little reason to suppose that it does not cross with others. Unlike the Arfak Six-wired Bird, the Superb Bird of Paradise is not restricted to the Vogelkop Peninsula. It occurs, at suitable altitudes, throughout New Guinea, in many places living alongside these other species. Some females of the Superb Bird are virtually identical (except for their smaller size) to females of Queen Carola's Six-wired Bird (*Parotia carolae*) and, bearing in mind the exotic colouring of males of this species, any crossing might produce some very spectacular results.

Figure 36 (Left)
Queen Carola's Six-wired Bird of Paradise (*Parotia carolae*) – male below, immature male, above. Hand-coloured lithograph by W. Hart from R. Bowdler Sharpe's *Monograph of the Paradiseidae* (London, 1891–8).

WILHELMINA'S BIRD OF PARADISE

Lophorina superba × *Diphyllodes magnificus?*

Lamprothorax wilhelminae Meyer, 1894, *Abhandlungen und Berichte des Koniglichen Zoologischen Museum zur Dresden*, 5, no.2, p.3.
Lophorina superba × *Diphyllodes magnificus* Stresemann, 1930, *Novitates Zoologicae*, 36, p.11.

DESCRIPTION

Lores and front part of cheeks velvety black; chin and upper throat bronze; sides of face purplish bronze; rest of head and neck purplish violet with feathers of hindneck blackish and forming a frill; throat purplish bronze; scapulars blackish with brownish gold centres to feathers; back and wings black with mixture of reddish brown feathers and some purple sheening; tail black with purplish gloss and two central feathers narrow, elongated and covered with steel green glitter; breast metallic bluish green; abdomen, thighs and under tail coverts black.

MEASUREMENTS

Length (excluding long central tail feathers) 230 mm (9 inches); wing 127–129 mm; tail (without central feathers) 70–73 mm; central tail feathers 129–148 mm; bill 35 mm; tarsus 35 mm.

PLACE OF ORIGIN

Arfak Mountains.

LOCATION OF SPECIMENS

Dresden, Leiden, New York.

Abh. Ber. Zool. Mus. Dresden. 1894/5. Nr. 2: Meyer, Vögel Ostind. Arch.

Lamprothorax wilhelminae n. sp.
Nat. Gr.

Plate XXX
Wilhelmina's Bird of Paradise.
Hand-coloured lithograph by Bruno
Geisler from *Abhandlungen und
Berichte des Königlichen Zoologischen
Museum zur Dresden* (1894–5), Pl.2.

Wilhelmina's Bird of Paradise

Erwin Stresemann (1889–1972) was among the most distinguished ornithologists of his time. In some respects he serves as a link between past and present. His career began in the period of the gentleman naturalist – often flamboyant and wildly eccentric characters – and drew to an end when a cooler, blander approach, generally built around formal biological training, had become fashionable. As a young man Stresemann left his native Germany to participate in the *Second Freiburg Moluccas Expedition* and it was during this adventure that he encountered tropical birds for the first time. A deep interest in the birds of the South Pacific never left him.

Stresemann's ornithological work was interrupted by two world wars, and although during both conflicts he dutifully served his country, he appears never to have lost sight of the basic principles of humanity. During World War I he saw active service with an artillery unit bogged down for three years on the Western Front between Verdun and Belfort. During World War II he was drafted into the *Luftwaffe* but was eventually exempted from service and spent the last half of the war preserving and

Figure 37
Erwin Stresemann (1889–1972)
being tattooed with a headhunter's
sign in Seram, 1911.

Figure 38
Ernst Hartert (1860–1933), the
Curator of Birds at Walter
Rothschild's Tring Museum.
Courtesy of The Hon. Miriam
Rothschild.

hiding precious books and specimens belonging to the Berlin Museum. It is recorded that during these years he performed many small acts of kindness for Allied prisoners of war.

Stresemann produced hundreds of papers on a wide range of ornithological subjects, and among these was his influential work on unusual birds of paradise. For publication of this paper he turned, quite naturally, to Walter Rothschild and his scientific journal *Novitates Zoologicae*. It seems that Stresemann never quite came to terms with the power and privilege enjoyed by the English lord, and in later years he showed a tendency to dismiss all of Rothschild's achievements as merely the products of that power. He apparently failed to appreciate Walter's great skill for organising the Tring Museum and discovering men of exceptional talent like Ernst Hartert and Karl Jordan to run the departments of ornithology and entomology. Walter was a phenomenal *animateur*. It was he, for instance, who encouraged Hartert to act as mentor for young researchers (such as Stresemann) and Walter himself liked nothing better than imparting his knowledge of natural history to an audience.

Stresemann was contemptuous of the curious lacunae in Walter's knowledge of hard science – a sphere in which he himself excelled – but although he did not realise it, his own unbridled admiration for Ernst Hartert was also admiration for the Tring scenario which was Walter's triumphant creation. Stresemann's relationship with the Tring Museum nevertheless proved more than satisfactory. Indeed, he made long visits, staying always with the Harterts. Ernst Hartert was for almost forty years Rothschild's curator and Stresemann became greatly attached to his fellow German, seeing himself very much in the role of pupil to the older ornithologist. Years after Hartert's death, Stresemann expressed the rather bizarre, yet quite touching, request that, when the time came, his own remains be interred with those of the man to whom he felt he owed so much; how seriously this request was made cannot, of course, be said. Quite apart from these sentimental aspects, the close connection with Tring was essential for Stresemann's work. Without the Museum's aid it would have been impossible to make any meaningful review of the lost birds of paradise. With Rothschild's incomparable collection at Stresemann's disposal, the task could at least be attempted (ironically, within two years of the publication of Stresemann's paper, Walter's great collection crossed the Atlantic and became the property of the American Museum of Natural History).

So it was that in 1930 the *Novitates Zoologicae* carried Stresemann's paper *Welche Paradiesvogelarten der Literatur sind Hybriden Ursprungs?* In this cleverly conceived and, at the time, quite revolutionary work, Stresemann set himself the task of resolving the mystery surrounding the lost birds of paradise. Ingeniously, he proposed a definite hybrid origin for all the forms then known. Stresemann's obvious accuracy in the majority of cases, coupled with his enormous academic prestige, ensured an almost complete acceptance of all these proposals among his peers.

The obvious weaknesses in his paper have remained largely uncommented upon. These weaknesses are two-fold. The first lies in Stresemann's dogged determination to provide a definitive solution to each particular case history. In some instances the nature of the available evidence simply will not allow this. The other shortcoming is Stresemann's use of what might be termed 'cryptic' taxonomy: often he states his conclusions with little or no discussion of the reasons behind them. His account of Wilhelmina's Bird of Paradise is a perfect example of this. Under the caption *Diphyllodes magnificus* × *Lophorina superba* he says:

> Nur 3 Exemplare bekannt: je eines in Dresden ('Arfak-Gebirge'), in Leiden ('Arfak-Gerbirge') und Tring (ohne Fundort). Ein sehr komplizierter Bastard. Kompromiss zwischen kurzen und äusserst stark verlängerten mittleren Schwanzfedern wei bei *Janthothorax*.

> Three examples are known: these are in Dresden (Arfak Mountains), Leiden (Arfak Mountains) and in Tring (place of origin unknown). This is a very complicated hybrid. There is a combination of shorter outer tail feathers and lengthened central tail feathers as in *Janthothorax*.

This short statement is Stresemann's entire published justification for invalidating a species that had been considered legitimate for a period of almost forty years. Only in

Plate XXXI
Magnificent Bird of Paradise
(*Diphyllodes magnificus*) – males
above left and below, female above
right. Hand-coloured lithograph by
J. Gould and W. Hart from J.
Gould's *Birds of New Guinea*
(London, 1875–88), Pl.22.

the caption heading the account is Stresemann's revolutionary proposition actually stated. The reference to *Janthothorax* (Bensbach's Bird of Paradise) is peculiarly misplaced and its quite irrelevent entry into the discussion, with so much of significance left unsaid, is bizarre.

Yet the case for the 'species' *Lamprothorax wilhelminae* actually being the hybrid Stresemann believed it to be is not without merit. The two birds proposed as parents – the Superb Bird of Paradise and the Magnificent Bird of Paradise – are both quite common New Guinea birds, so there is no reason why they should not regularly come into contact.

Occupying a fairly central position in the systematics of the Paradiseidae, the Superb Bird of Paradise has, conceivably, the ability to interact with a comparatively large number of other species. From the geographical point of view it is perfectly placed to do so for it lives throughout much of New Guinea. Similarly its altitudinal range brings it into contact with birds of the lower hills and also with those that live at considerably higher levels. As far as interaction with the Magnificent Bird of Paradise is concerned, the two species can come into contact at the upper limits of the Magnificent Bird's altitudinal range. Generally, these birds replace one another altitudinally and the most likely cross would involve female Superbs (with their tendency to favour the lower heights) and male Magnificents, but this, of course, need not necessarily be the case. The males of the two species are markedly different in appearance, so much so that the possibility of hybridisation may seem remote, but from the ethological viewpoint there may be little discrepancy between them; certainly their respective females are quite similar.

The evidence provided by the three specimens of Wilhelmina's Bird of Paradise is obviously crucial to the case. But what might be expected in a cross between two birds in which the male of one species is predominantly yellow and the male of the other mostly black? Wilhelmina's Bird of Paradise certainly shows characteristics that might be interpreted as intermediate, but these are also features that could have arisen quite independently. The structure of the feathering of the head is similar to that shown in the Magnificent but the colour is different. The beautiful metallic bluish green of the breast is similar in colouring to the Superb Bird's extravagant ornamental shield but more like the Magnificent's breast pad in shape. The tail is black with purple sheening and the two central tail feathers are straight, narrow, elongated and shimmer with bluish green iridescence; the Superb Bird has a velvet black tail of even length and the Magnificent's tail is brown with two wire-like, sharply curved central retrices. The Magnificent Bird of Paradise has elongated scapulars of gold, Wilhelmina's has shorter blackish scapulars that have brownish gold centres. Such features might be considered coincidental or they may point, as conjectured, to a hybrid origin. Taking all factors into account, and bearing in mind particularly the tendency of the Paradiseidae to produce occasional crosses, the probability is that this is the hybrid stated.

The form was first described by A.B. Meyer in 1894 from a specimen received at the Dresden Museum. During the same year another was acquired by the Leiden Museum. Both these examples show some signs of immaturity. Four years later Walter Rothschild received a specimen sent by Renesse van Duivenbode, and this bird is now in New York.

The fact that two of the known specimens are alleged to have come from the Arfak Mountains is probably not of any great significance. It is perhaps merely a reflection of the large number of trade skins taken from this particular area during the period when the bird came to attention. If the form is a valid species, however, some part of the Arfak Mountains would presumably represent its home grounds.

THE KING OF HOLLAND'S BIRD OF PARADISE

Diphyllodes magnificus × *Cicinnurus regius*

Diphyllodes gulielmi III Meyer, 1875, *Der Zoologischer Garten*, 16, p.29.

Rhipidornis guglielmi tertii Salvadori, 1876, *Ann. Mus. Genova*, 9, p.192.

Rhipidornis gulielmi tertii Sharpe, 1893, *Monograph of the Paradiseidae*, pt.2.

Rhipidornis gulielmi tertii Meyer, 1898, *Abhandlungen und Berichte des Koniglichen Zoologischen Museums zur Dresden*, 8, no.2, p.41.

Diphyllodes gulielmi tertii Rothschild, 1898, *Das Tierreich – Aves*, lief 2, p.25.

Diphyllodes magnificus × *Cicinnurus regius* Stresemann, 1930, *Novitates Zoologicae*, 36, p.7.

DESCRIPTION

Head and neck orange red (sometimes richer red, sometimes more brownish), most individuals (not all) with dark spot over each eye as in *Cicinnurus regius*; nape caped with rich orange; upper back blood red; lower back golden olive; wings orange; tail brown; chin and throat orange brown; breast shield iridescent green terminating in band of turquoise-tipped feathers and flanked by tufts of axe-shaped purplish brown feathers with scythe-shaped emerald green tips; abdomen brownish to sandy yellow, undertail coverts with creamish tinting; central retrices long, wire-like and lyre-shaped with green vanes showing towards ends.

MEASUREMENTS

Length 175 mm (7 inches); wing 108 mm; tail 39 mm; bill 20 mm; tarsus 30 mm.

PLACE OF ORIGIN

Widely separated localities of lowland New Guinea.

LOCATION OF SPECIMENS

Amsterdam, Berlin, Dresden, Edinburgh, Leiden, Liverpool, London (Tring), New York – twelve specimens, Paris, Sydney, Warsaw.

Plate XXXII
King of Holland's Bird of Paradise.
Hand-coloured lithograph by J.
Gould and W. Hart from J. Gould's
Birds of New Guinea (London,
1875–88), Pl.21.

DIPHYLLODES GULIELMI, III, *Meyer.*

J. Gould & W. Hart del. et lith.   Walter imp.

The King of Holland's Bird of Paradise

The King of Holland's Bird of Paradise is an avian jewel, perhaps the most exquisitely perfect of all the smaller paradise birds. It is also almost certainly a hybrid resulting from mating between the King Bird of Paradise (*Cicinnurus regius*) and the Magnificent (*Diphyllodes magnificus*), its own remarkable plumage being clearly stamped with marks of both assumed parent birds. More than two dozen preserved specimens exist, making this a comparatively common 'lost' form, and these are scattered among the museum collections of many countries. Some have been carefully prepared and are well looked after. For others this is not the case, yet even in the most pitiful of museum relics the astonishing gem-like quality of the bird as it must have appeared in life is quite apparent.

The first specimens to come to light – a pair of trade skins, male and female, preserved by natives – were purchased, probably in 1874, in Salawati (an island off the western end of New Guinea) from the captain of a Celebes boat. Their purchaser was one S.C.T. van Musschenbroek, an officer of the Dutch East Indian Service, a gentleman sufficiently well-versed in natural history matters to recognise that he had acquired something new to science. Van Musschenbroek, therefore, did two things. He sent a description of his birds to a friend in Europe, Baron von Rosenberg, requesting that this description be published and the birds given the scientific name *Diphyllodes gulielmi III* in honour of the King of Holland. The birds themselves he forwarded to the Dresden Museum and the care of A.B. Meyer, at this time a leading bird of paradise specialist.

Both men seem to have kept good faith with van Musschenbroek (which is not always the way of things in these matters), doing their best to comply with his wishes. Accordingly, two virtually identical descriptions of his birds were published, one by von Rosenberg, the other by Meyer. By curious coincidence these two descriptions were placed in the very same journal, the *Zoologischer Garten*, for the same month, January 1875, and they even managed to occupy succeeding pages.

The two birds remained for a year or so at the Dresden Museum and then, much to Meyer's despair, they were removed. He plaintively narrated the circumstances, and his attempts to recover them, as follows:

> I one day in the year 1877 received a telegram from van Musschenbroek, who had returned home in 1876, telling me that he wished to show the birds to King William III. I sent the specimens to him and never saw them again. They remained in the hands of the King, and we never succeeded in recovering these types for science, though supported by the late Professor Schlegel of Leyden; but after van Musschenbroek's death, in the year 1883, the King of the Netherlands delivered the specimens to the Museum of the Zoological Society of Amsterdam, where they will probably remain.

Meyer's prediction proved accurate. Van Musschenbroek's birds remain in Holland to this day and are now held by the Institute voor Taxonomische Zoologie, Universiteit van Amsterdam, the male numbered ZMA 782 and the female ZMA 783.

Figure 39
William III, King of Holland
(1817–1890).

Plate XXXIII
A King of Holland's Bird of Paradise
– stuffed.

Plate XXXIV
Mr Whiteley's bird. A cabinet skin
now in the collection of the British
Museum (Natural History).

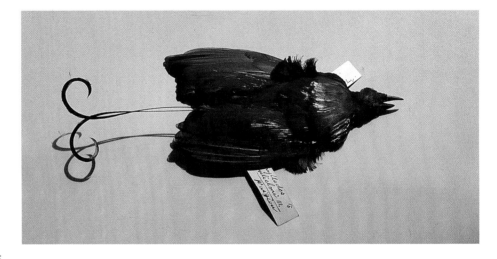

Plate XXXV
(Facing page), King Bird of Paradise
(*Cicinnurus regius*) – adult male top
and bottom, immature male centre
left, female centre right. Hand-
coloured lithograph by J. Wolf and
J. Smit from D.G. Elliot's *Monograph
of the Paradiseidae* (London, 1873),
Pl.16.

There is considerable doubt over whether or not this female has been correctly
assigned. Most specialists who see it believe it to be simply an unmixed female
Magnificent Bird of Paradise, and it presumably became associated with its extraordinary male companion for no better reason than that the two were purchased
together as a job lot. However this may be, both specimens are now housed together

J.Wolf. & J.Smit del.et.lith.

CICINNURUS REGIUS

M.& N.Hanhart imp

in the Institute's skin collection after being long exhibited in a case for mounted birds. Curiously, this former display of simple skins 're-made' into fully stuffed-up birds necessitated a rather bizarre additional act of hybridisation, this one performed by an unnamed taxidermist at an unknown date. The male, as originally acquired by van Musschenbroek, was without legs, a circumstance that often occured with native-prepared skins. In order to give his display some degree of acceptability, the anonymous taxidermist diluted the purity of the little male hybrid still further, by grafting onto it the legs of a starling!

Although unique when put into the care of the King of Holland, the little male bird – soon to be given the starling legs – did not remain so for long. A trade skin came into the possession of a Monsieur M.A. Bouvier of Paris who disposed of it to the Warsaw Museum. Before travelling east, however, this particular individual was sent on loan to John Gould and served as the model for the illustration (*see* p. 95) published in his *Birds of New Guinea* (1875–88). Another was received by a Mr Whiteley

Figure 40
John Gould (1804–1881), artist,
author, producer of fine books and
avid collector of birds.

of Woolwich in south London, and this example was exhibited before the Zoological Society on 1 May 1883. During the same year it was acquired by the British Museum where it is still to be found, in battered condition but remaining, somehow, exquisitely beautiful.

By the time Richard Bowdler Sharpe produced his *Monograph of the Paradiseidae* (1891–8), he knew of no fewer than three specimens in the hands of a single collector – Walter Rothschild, perhaps the most dedicated horder of stuffed birds and animals who ever lived. By the end of his collecting days, Rothschild had amassed no fewer than ten examples of the King of Holland's Bird of Paradise.

The gradual rise in the number of native-killed and preserved specimens continued even long after the general decline in plume-hunting but still, it seems, no ornithologist has encountered a living example. Although the majority of individuals have reached museums without reliable locality data, the data present with the remainder indicates that this bird of paradise has been procured from widely separated localities. This, of course, is what might be expected in a form that is the hybrid of two common and widespread species with ranges that overlap in many places. To strengthen this hybrid hypothesis it can be pointed out that the two proposed parent species are particularly closely related (Coates, 1990, for instance, unites them in the same genus – *Cicinnurus*) and aspects of their sexual display and their display songs are remarkably similar.

Assuming then that the King of Holland's Bird of Paradise is a hybrid, it is perhaps not too much to hope, even to expect, that this beautiful product of illicit matings still occurs from time to time on the wild hillsides of lowland New Guinea.

THE LYRE-TAILED KING

Cicinnurus regius × *Diphyllodes magnificus?*

Cicinnurus lyogyrus Currie, 1900, *Proc. US Nat. Museum*, 22, p.497.

Cicinnurus goodfellowi Ogilvie-Grant, 1907, *Bulletin of the British Ornithologists' Club*, 19, p.39.

Cicinnurus regius × *Rhipidornis gulielmi tertii* Rothschild, 1911, *Ibis,* p.362.

Cicinnurus regius × *Diphyllodes magnificus* Stresemann, 1930, *Novitates Zoologicae*, 36, p.7.

Cicinnurus lyrogyrus Mayr, 1941, *List of New Guinea Birds*, p.182.

DESCRIPTION

All of head, throat, neck, back, wings and tail coverts bright orange crimson, but upper surface of tail itself brownish; upper breast shows broad band of deep iridescent green (three times as broad as that of typical king birds); rest of underparts white; axe-shaped pectoral tufts tipped green; wire-like central retrices long and lyre-shaped showing iridescent green vanes at ends; small black spot over eye; iris dark brown (*goodfellowi*); feet dark cobalt blue (*goodfellowi*); bill yellow (*goodfellowi*).

MEASUREMENTS

C. lyogyrus: length 170 mm (6½ inches); wing 100 mm; tail 35 mm; bill 22 mm; tarsus 30 mm.

C. goodfellowi: length 170 mm (6½ inches); wing 102 mm; tail 35 mm; bill 24 mm; tarsus 32 mm.

PLACE OF ORIGIN

Cyclops Mountains, northern Irian Jaya.

LOCATION OF SPECIMENS

Berlin, London (Tring), Washington.

Plate XXXVI
Lyre-tailed King. Oil painting by
Errol Fuller.

The Lyre-Tailed King

The King Bird of Paradise (*Cicinnurus regius*) is a common New Guinea species likely to be found in most lowland areas of the great island and also on some offshore isles. One of its most striking and individual features is a peculiar, tight coiling of the two central tail feathers at their ends. Although the species has been split into six sub-species, there is no appreciable variation in this extraordinary feature from one end of New Guinea to the other.

On at least three occasions, however, aberrant king birds have been found. Not only do these birds show less tightly coiled tails, their beautiful emerald green breast bands are very much broader than those of more regular individuals. What this means is unclear. Whether they are freaks, hybrids or, as two of them were apparently found in the same range of mountains, members of a clearly marked race, remains uncertain.

The first of these curious birds – a specimen received in Washington without locality data from a Monsieur Boucard – was noticed by Rolla P. Currie in 1900 and put in the type collection of the US National Museum (no. 124628). Principally on account of lyre-shaped central tail feathers, but also because of the broadness of the green breast band and the reduced length of the axe-shaped pectoral plumes, Currie felt justified in erecting a new species. This he named *Cicinnurus lyogyrus* but, lapsing unaccountably, he managed to supply in his description a set of measurements wholly inappropriate for the bird in question (wing 200 mm rather than 100 mm; tail 78 mm rather than 35 mm; bill 42 mm rather than 22 mm; tarsus 50 mm rather than 30 mm). Curiously, this is not the only error of this kind associated with *lyogyrus*. Some writers (including Ernst Mayr) are unable to resist the temptation of slipping an 'r' into the name, making *lyrogyrus* instead of *lyogyrus*.

In August 1906, six years after Currie described his new species, the explorer Walter Goodfellow took a seemingly very similar bird at an altitude of 3,000 feet (930 metres) in the Cyclops Mountains, northern New Guinea. The retrice ends of this particular bird were, however, a little less unfurled than those of *lyogyrus* and so, during the following year, W.R. Ogilvie-Grant made this individual the type of another new 'species' – *Cicinnurus goodfellowi*.

In 1923 yet another aberrant king bird was found, and it was acquired by Erwin Stresemann for the Berlin Museum. It, too, apparently came from the Cyclops Mountains and Stresemann, naturally, correlated his example with Ogilvie-Grant's *goodfellowi*.

Exactly how *goodfellowi* and *lyogyrus* relate to one another remains uncertain. Equally uncertain is the way in which they relate to the orthodox King Bird. To account for the uncurling of the central retrices and the broadening of the breast band, the action of hybridisation is usually proposed. Both forms are usually listed as hybrids of the King Bird and the Magnificent Bird of Paradise (*Diphyllodes magnificus*), representing the reciprocal cross to that which produces the King of Holland's Bird of Paradise.

This is perhaps the safest consideration but other suggestions have been made. Because of the obvious closeness to the King Bird, and also the seeming distance from the Magnificent, Rothschild (1911) considered that these divergent individuals were the result of regular kings back-crossing with their own – alleged – hybrid, the King of Holland's Bird. Although this is possible, it seems unlikely on statistical grounds alone.

It is, of course, curious that both specimens of *goodfellowi* appear to have derived from the Cyclops Mountains. Why this should be so is unclear, for both the King and the Magnificent live side by side in many of the lower parts of New Guinea so their hybrids might be expected in any of these places. It must be assumed, therefore, that some unknown condition operating in the Cyclops Mountains particularly favours the production of this form.

RUYS' BIRD OF PARADISE

Diphyllodes magnificus × *Paradisea minor?*

Neoparadisea ruysi van Oort, 1906, *Notes Leyden Museum*, 28, p.129.
Diphyllodes magnifica magnifica × *Paradisea minor minor* Stresemann, 1930, *Novitates Zoologicae*, 36, p.8.

DESCRIPTION

Chin and throat black with purple green gloss; lower neck blackish brown with purplish blue gloss; breast cushion deep brownish blue purple; abdomen and undertail coverts blackish brown, the latter with lighter centres; tuft of loose feathers on flanks sooty brown with whitish brown barbs at distal end; forehead greenish black; head and upper neck brownish yellow with greenish black margins to feathers becoming more orange brown on lower neck; rump and upper tail coverts olive brown; tail brown with purplish gloss; wings brown with purplish blue gloss; legs dull bluish black.

MEASUREMENTS

Length 290 mm (11½ inches); wing 150 mm; tail 90 mm (central retrices 360 mm); lower mandible (upper mandible broken) 32 mm; tarsus 42 mm.

PLACE OF ORIGIN

Near Warsembo (west coast of Geelvink Bay).

Plate XXXVII
Ruys' Birds of Paradise. Oil painting
by Errol Fuller.

LOCATION OF SPECIMEN

Leiden.

Ruys' Bird of Paradise

During August – or, perhaps, September – of 1905, Papuan hunters, working their way through the vasts lowland forests that fringe the Geelvink Bay, collected an altogether extraordinary bird the like of which has not been seen since. Their location at the time of the find can be pinpointed almost exactly. It was close to Warsembo on the west coast of the Geelvink Bay, almost opposite the island of Amberspoon.

The bird became the property of a Mr H. Ruys who was nearing the end of a four-year stay in what was then Dutch New Guinea (now Irian Jaya). On Ruys' return to Holland he presented a collection of bird of paradise skins to the Leiden Museum and included among it a rare example of the King of Holland's Bird of Paradise and the unique bird taken by the hunters of Warsembo. In some recognition of this act, Dr E.D. van Oort named the new treasure of the Leiden Museum *Neoparadisea ruysi*. Unique and puzzling in 1905, Ruys' bird remains so today.

Whatever its true nature, there seems a definite connection with the birds of the genus *Paradisea*. The general size and structure, the long wire-like central retrices and a suggestion of flank plumes all point in this direction. Yet the overall appearance is

Figure 41
Ruys' Bird of Paradise – the unique specimen in the Leiden Museum. Courtesy of the Rijksmuseum van Natuurlijke Historie, Leiden.

aberrant and the fact that the skin is not that of a fully mature individual serves only further to confuse the issue. In his original description van Oort pointed out seeming similarities with the genus *Paradisea* and also with the genus *Diphyllodes*. Consequently, it was natural that Erwin Stresemann (1930) should consider Ruys' bird to be the hybrid of the Lesser Bird of Paradise (*Paradisea minor*) and the Magnificent (*Diphyllodes magnificus*).

The mystery bird is altogether larger than the Magnificent Bird of Paradise. Its bill is correspondingly bigger but has been described as similar in shape to the beak of the smaller bird. How this particular description could be made is unclear for the upper mandible of Ruys' bird is badly broken. The feather structure on the nape suggests, perhaps, the Magnificent's cape and ruff, and the deep purple breast cushion might be a distant reflection of the green breast cushion of the putative parent. Whether or not these rather vague connections add up to proof of the bird's hybrid origin is, ultimately, a matter of opinion. The probability of the Lesser Bird of Paradise mating with the very much smaller Magnificent does not, after all, seem very great, particularly as the smaller species has evolved a breeding system that in certain respects approaches that of the bower birds.

The two suggested parent species share much territory in northern New Guinea; even altitudinally they have similar preferences – heights below 5,200 feet (1,600 metres). Hybrids between them could, therefore, turn up in any of the hundreds of square miles they jointly occupy. Presumably, the unique nature of Ruys' Bird of Paradise is an indication that such crosses, assuming they do actually occur, happen only very rarely.

Figure 42
The entrance to Leiden Museum, a research institution that is not open to the public.

BENSBACH'S BIRD OF PARADISE

Janthothorax bensbachi Büttikofer, 1894

Janthothorax bensbachi Büttikofer, 1894, *Notes Leyden Museum*, 16, p.163.
Paradisea minor × *Ptilorhis magnifica* Stresemann, 1930, *Novitates Zoologicae*, 36, p.10.

DESCRIPTION
Crown metallic green with bronze reflections; sides of face and upper throat metallic green, more bronze on face, more blue on throat; lower throat bronze green with purplish reflections; breast purplish black; abdomen brownish black glossed purple; upper back purplish black; lower back and rump brown; wing coverts sandy brown, rest of wings brownish black glossed metallic green; tail brown but two central feathers green, and much longer and narrower than others; flank plumes dark brown; bill and feet black; iris (according to Bensbach) red.

MEASUREMENTS
Length 330 mm (13 inches); wing 170 mm; tail 120 mm (long central tail feathers 204 mm); bill 44 mm; tarsus 40 mm.

Plate XXXVIII
Bensbach's Bird of Paradise. Hand-coloured lithograph by J.G. Keulemans and W. Hart (after a painting by Keulemans) from R. Bowdler Sharpe's *Monograph of the Paradiseidae* (London, 1891–8), Pl.8.

PLACE OF ORIGIN
Arfak Mountains, north-west New Guinea.

LOCATION OF SPECIMEN
Leiden.

IANTHOTHORAX BENZBACHI, *Büttik.*

J.G.Keulemans & Hart del. et lith.

Mintern Bros.imp.

Bensbach's Bird of Paradise

Nachum die Deutung von *Janthothorax mirabilis* sichergestellt ist, kann man bei Prüfung des im Leidener Museums aufbewahrten Unikums von *J. bensbachi* nicht in Zweifel darüber bleiben, dass hier das Produkt einer Kreuzung von *Paradisea minor* and *Ptiloris magnificus* vorliegt.

When the meaning of *Janthothorax mirabilis* [the Wonderful Bird of Paradise] has been made clear, one can, by examining the single example of *J. bensbachi* [Bensbach's Bird of Paradise] in the Leiden Museum, remain in no doubt that it is the hybrid of *Paradisea minor* [Lesser Bird of Paradise] and *Ptiloris magnificus* [Magnificent Rifle Bird].

This single, uneasy sentence, written by Erwin Stresemann in 1930, was enough to convince ornithologists the world over that *Janthothorax bensbachi* should be removed from the list of bird species. It might be expected that any widespread critical acceptance of such an idea would depend on a clear additional explanation. What extra insight Stresemann gave his readers comes in a second, and final, remark:

Völlig geschwärzte Untersite und die Qualität des Schillers an verschiedenen Regionen des Gefieders schliessen *Seleucidis* aus und zeugen für *Ptiloris*.

Completely blackened undersides and the quality of shimmer in various parts of the plumage, exclude *Seleucidis* [Twelve-wired Bird of Paradise] and point towards *Ptiloris* [Magnificent Rifle Bird].

Possibly, Bensbach's Bird of Paradise is exactly what Stresemann believed it to be, but his cryptic explanation is unsatisfactory and its virtually unquestioned acceptance is perplexing. Quite why blackish underparts should point to a rifle bird is unclear; no less than twenty-one bird of paradise species show this particular feature. Stresemann's vague remark on the 'quality of shimmer' is no more helpful, one of the trademarks of birds of paradise being their bewildering array of shimmers, glosses, sheens and iridescent glows. The introduction of another controversial form – *mirabilis*, the Wonderful Bird – to clarify the reasoning, serves only to obscure it further.

Bensbach's Bird of Paradise can be considered either a hybrid or a lost, possibly extinct, species. As with many lost birds of paradise, the difficulty with Bensbach's is that evaluation must be made from the specimen alone without the aid of additional information. The type specimen is unique and was presented in 1894 to the Leiden Museum by Mr J. Bensbach, the Dutch Resident at Ternate. It came to Europe with only the vaguest, and possibly quite unreliable, locality data: the Arfak Mountains, north-west New Guinea. An extra complication is that this sole example does not seem quite mature, so the appearance of the fully adult bird is not really known.

If it is a hybrid, its parentage is by no means certain to be that proposed by

Stresemann. Because the specimen bears no unequivocal marks in its plumage, other species with compatible ranges might make equally credible parents (a six-wired bird might, for example, substitute for the rifle bird). Stresemann's argument for the Magnificent Rifle Bird and the Lesser Bird of Paradise seems to be inspired as much by his use of other possible combinations to account for other problematical forms, as by any positive evidence incriminating these two particular species. It might even be suggested that the major reason for supposing *benshachi* a hybrid is that other unusual birds of paradise can be demonstrated to be so.

Although the hybrid diagnosis may eventually be proved correct, it is unsafe. There are a surprisingly large number of unchallenged, yet essentially mysterious, bird species known from just a single encounter with ornithological science. Until such time as its illegitimacy is clearly revealed, it is inconsistent to exclude *Janthothorax benshachi* from this number.

Figure 43
The only known specimen of Bensbach's Bird of Paradise. Courtesy of the Rijksmuseum van Natuurlijke Historie, Leiden.

THE WONDERFUL BIRD OF PARADISE

Paradisea minor × Seleucidis melanoleuca?

Paradisea mirabilis Reichenow, 1901, *Orn. Monatsber.*, 9, p.186.
Janthothorax mirabilis Rothschild, 1903, *Bulletin of the British Ornithologists' Club*, 13, p.31.
Paradisea minor × Seleucides nigricans Stresemann, 1930, *Novitates Zoologicae*, 36, p.9.
Quesoparens mirabilis Iredale, 1950, *Birds of Paradise and Bower Birds*, p.52.

DESCRIPTION
Head, throat and upper back blackish blue; lower part of back dirty yellowish grey flecked with deep blue; wings brown; tail brown but with turquoise-sheened, narrow, pointed central retrices approximately 20 mm longer than other features; breast and upper abdomen velvety purplish brown; lower abdomen yellowish grey; long flank plumes whitish grey in front, chocolate brown behind; bill long and sturdy.

MEASUREMENTS
Length 330 mm (13 inches); wing 186 mm; tail 120 mm (with central retrices 20 mm longer); bill 50 mm; tarsus 45 mm.

PLACE OF ORIGIN
Arfak Mountains, north-west New Guinea; Madang, northern Papua.

LOCATION OF SPECIMENS
New York – four specimens Bogor (Java).

Journ. f. Ornith. 1902.

Taf. I.

²/₅ n. Gr.

Paradisea mirabilis Rhw.

Plate XXXIX
The Wonderful Bird of Paradise.
Hand-coloured lithograph by Bruno
Geisler from the *Journal für
Ornithologie* (1902), Pl.1.

The Wonderful Bird of Paradise

Situated on the Astrolabe Bay in what is now northern Papua is the town of Madang, once one of the headquarters of the old plume trade. During the first decade of the twentieth century thousands of plume birds were shipped from this port to Europe to supply the requirements of the fashion industry. Such were the numbers exported that, locally at least, birds of paradise were virtually eliminated. From here, or to be more precise from Friedrich-Wilhelmshafen (the area was at that time part of German New Guinea and Madang was suitably named), came, in 1901, a quite remarkable trade skin.

When viewed from the front, the long plumes were a dirty whitish colour but from behind they were chocolate brown. Above the plumes the pattern was reversed: the breast was brown, the back yellowish grey. For description, the specimen was given to Anton Reichenow, a specialist in African birds and, at the time, Director of the Berlin Museum. Its great peculiarity caused Reichenow to suspect a hybrid origin but, even so, he named the bird as a full species: *Paradisea mirabilis* – the Wonderful Bird of Paradise.

Sharing the destiny of many other rare birds of paradise, *mirabilis* quickly became the property of Walter Rothschild, and in his museum it was soon joined by two similarly 'wonderful' individuals. Both of these were believed to come from an entirely different locality to the first specimen, the mode of their preparation being that employed by native collectors of the Arfak Mountains, a region situated hundreds of miles to the west of Madang. Whether or not this assumption of an Arfak locality can be relied upon is not entirely clear, however. A fourth example subsequently came to light and it exists at the American Museum of Natural History where, coincidentally, the first three specimens are now also to be found, having been purchased by the Museum along with much else of the Rothschild collection.

Just as the precise places of origin are uncertain, similarly unclear is the exact status of these strange creatures. Certainly they carry cryptic signs in their plumage to confuse even the most experienced examiner. When Erwin Stresemann (1930) reviewed them as part of his survey of unusual birds of paradise, he concluded that they were the results of matings between the Lesser Bird of Paradise (*Paradisea minor*) and the Twelve-wired (*Seleucidis melanoleuca*). This judgement, shrewdly based upon plumage characteristics and locality data of specimens, is likely to be correct even though the basic concept of such a cross seems rather extraordinary. Along with its conceptual clumsiness, however, the idea hardly explains some quite significant plumage peculiarities. The dirty white and brown colour of the ornamental flank plumes (a characteristic just possibly reflecting a stage in the plume development of the wired bird's immature male) is a feature that might be more understandable if, for instance, the Magnificent Rifle Bird (*Ptiloris magnificus*) were to substitute for the Twelve-wired Bird. This substitution is not in conflict with the assumed places of origin for the 'wonderful birds' but it hardly brings the problem into clear focus and certainly the birds themselves look more like the hybrids that Stresemann suggested.

Unless additional evidence comes to light it seems correct to suppose that the Lesser Bird of Paradise interacts with the Twelve-wired to produce the Wonderful.

I have found out a gift for my fair-
'Tis a paradise plume for her hat;
   The naturalists think
   The bird's getting extinct;
She will like it the better for that.

I have found out a gift for my fair-
An owl's head to put in her hat;
   There is not a bird
   More useful I've heard;
But my sweet, she won't mind about that.

I have found out a gift for my fair-
A kingfisher's skin laid out flat;
   It's a bird that don't sing
   And a quite worthless thing
Except to be stuck in a hat.

I have found out a gift for my fair-
A white egret's plume for her hat;
   T'was the honeymoon crest
   Of a bird on its nest;
But she won't care a rap about that.

I have found out a gift for my fair-
A pair of stork legs- think of that!
   If they do look absurd
   that's the fault of the bird,
Not to grow legs more fit for a hat.

Figures 44 and 45
A Victorian cartoon poking fun at
the plume and fashion trade,
together with verses that
accompanied it. The cartoon's
caption was 'A Killing Hat'.

'PARADISEA MIXTA'

Paradisea minor × *Paradisea raggiana*

Paradisea mixta Rothschild, 1921, *Bulletin of the British Ornithologists' Club*, 41, p.127.
Paradisea minor finschi × *Paradisea apoda augustae-victoriae* Stresemann, 1930, *Novitates Zoologicae*, 36, p.14.

DESCRIPTION

Lores and chin black glossed green; throat iridescent bottle green; rest of head, nape, most of black and upper wing coverts yellow; remainder of wings brown; tail brown; yellow collar almost indistinguishable; velvet breast cushion dark brown; rest of underparts lighter brown; flank plumes yellow; becoming more cinnamon towards tips; central retrices long and wire-like.

MEASUREMENTS

Length (excluding plumes) 350 mm (14 inches); wing 190 mm; tail 135 mm; bill 36 mm; tarsus 48 mm.

PLACE OF ORIGIN

Headwaters of the Ramu River, Papua New Guinea.

LOCATION OF SPECIMENS

London (Tring), New York.

Plate XXXX
'Paradisea mixta' with (left) female Greater Bird of Paradise (*Paradisea apoda*). Oil painting by Errol Fuller.

118

'Paradisea Mixta'

Without a word of warning, spears streamed our way. Ambush! Ateliwa got one right through his belly and it came out low down his back . . . I jumped behind a tree, with my revolver in my hand. All my other boys, instead of staying there and firing, threw their packs away and ran down the red clay mountainside.

I fired as soon as I could and hit one of the raiders right in the neck. He dropped . . . I fired twice more and that was the end of that . . . I grabbed my knapsack . . . and hobbled after my boys as fast as I could. They were sitting in the next clearing, having gone as far as they could run . . . It was dusk and I could hear the *garrumuts*. You could hear . . . voices on all sides talking, and they sounded ominous.

It started to rain – with an equatorial madness. We had nothing to eat, not a thing, we were high up and cold. My foot hurt, and I feared infection. My malaria was working in me hard. I was freezing and sweating at the same time.

Throughout the night the *garrumuts* dinned in our ears. Crocodile-skin tom toms kept going, sometimes loud, sometimes softer.

I stayed awake. I had time to think and listen and feel fear. I could picture myself with spears through me, impaled, de-gutted, as I had seen others . . . Shivering and shaking, I passed my most terrifying night in New Guinea.

In the morning the drum sounds ceased. We struggled down, falling, sliding, cursing, sweating, to the . . . coast.

At Salamaua I was arrested and charged with murder.

It might be thought that this extract is taken from a thrill-a-page adventure yarn, written to enthral Edwardian adolescents and make them yearn for far-off places and outrageous acts of derring-do. Alternatively, it could come, perhaps, from the heavily fictionalised memoirs of a roguish white-hunter and teller of tall tales, looking to enhance the mystique of his profession. In fact the passage comes from *My Wicked, Wicked Ways*, the autobiography of Errol Flynn. It is also, apparently, a more or less true account of events that actually happened.

Before finding stardom in Hollywood, Flynn had been something of a real-life swashbuckler and had spent several years drifting the South Seas in search of fortune and adventure. More than once he had washed up in New Guinea hoping for more of the fortune and less of the adventure, and getting exactly the opposite. On one visit he was indeed imprisoned, and then tried, for the killing of a Papuan, and this account is his own explanation of the circumstances surrounding the event.

Flynn was always attracted to the oddities of natural history. He claimed, for instance, to have helped his father take live platypuses from Australia to England. This happens to be a feat that all recognised zoological sources agree has never been accomplished. Whether Errol's story is true or not, no one really knows; it is just possible that the achievement went unrecorded by anyone other than the

Figure 46
Errol Flynn (1909–59) – dressed for adventure!

Flynns. Certainly Flynn the younger claimed no great glory for his part in it; in fact he acknowledged bringing near disaster to the entire enterprise. The platypuses were restricted to a diet of worms during the long voyage but Errol, apparently feeling sorry for them, decided to vary the menu. When the ship called at Durban, the greatest swashbuckler of them all managed to locate a supply of tadpoles and secretly slipped some into the tank containing his father's duckbills. That night two of the five platypuses were found floating feet up! According to Flynn, the remaining three made it all the way to London.

It was not primarily the study of natural history that took the then unknown Tasmanian to New Guinea, however. He was lured by the prospect of finding gold. But natural history stayed at the back of his mind, for he believed, quite perversely, that if gold proved elusive he could make a fortune in the plume trade:

> It is . . . amazing . . . to see a flock of wild birds of paradise. They swoop . . . into one tree, with their flowing tails, and their colours gold and an emerald green that sparkles. The shape and design of this bird is beautiful: a small head, a slender, delicate neck, and a leaflike blade coming down to a blaze of colour into the body. They fly very gracefully, though not fast . . . but the noise that comes from these creatures is raucous, dissonant . . . it shrills through your head, so that something of the beauty of the bird is taken away.

As everybody knows, neither gold nor birds of paradise were to form the basis of Errol's fortune, but his expectations reflected the hopes of many young adventurers of the time, even though the heyday of plume-hunting was by then long over.

Always it was the plume birds – Greater, Lesser and Count Raggi's – that were the main attraction, and the young Flynn's belief in their financial value provides a considerable insight into the intensity with which they were pursued. This intensity of persecution – resulting, as it did, in countless thousands of specimens of these three species being exported to Europe and America – had at least two quite unexpected consequences. Firstly, the birds' numbers did not appear to decrease significantly. This is yet another instance of the fact that hunting, distasteful though it may be, is not usually the prime cause of the destruction of species. For the vast majority of species, the greater threat lies in the destruction of the environment in which they live. Secondly, the huge numbers of specimens available for examination meant that even the minutest variations in plumage could be thoroughly studied and conclusions formed on the basis of this study. With museums having literally hundreds of specimens at their disposal, interested parties could match up a series and create new species or sub-species, often based on relatively insignificant differences of plumage, at a fairly bewildering rate. For many years the systematics of the genus *Paradisea* were horribly confusing.

One anomalous form that came to light from the study of museum specimens is known as *Paradisea mixta* and was first identified by Walter Rothschild in 1921, just a few years before Errol Flynn made his entrance on to the New Guinea stage. Walter formally described *Paradisea mixta* as a new species in the *Bulletin of the British Ornithologists' Club*. It can be distinguished from other plume birds of paradise by its combination of yellow flank plumes, yellow shoulder bar and deep velvet brown breast cushion. Not completely convinced by the status he was conferring, Rothschild appended a note to his description:

> The bird may be a hybrid between *minor* [Lesser Bird of Paradise] and *novae-guinea* [Greater Bird of Paradise] but it is not probable.

Time has shown that the hybrid assumption is, in fact, correct but that only one of the forms mentioned by Rothschild as a possible parent is actually involved. Stresemann (1930) thought *Paradisea mixta* the product of one of the sub-species of the Lesser Bird of Paradise (*Paradisea minor finschi*) and a sub-species of Count Raggi's Bird of Paradise (*Paradisea raggiana augustaevictoriae*). This seems to be the case.

The two parent species come into contact along several fronts. Stresemann remarked that hybrids could have originated from the Finisterre Mountains or the upper courses of the Ramu River. E.T. Gilliard, in his important study *Birds of Paradise and Bower Birds* (1969), asserts positively that 'mixta' is known from 'the headwaters of the Ramu River (at the Uria River)'. The same writer mentions a, presumably, similar hybrid that occurs at the upper edge of the Baiyer Valley. Here in the pass between the Baiyer River system and the Wahgi Valley quite extensive deforestation has occurred and Count Raggi's Bird has been able to force its way from the Wahgi into the Baiyer Valley to come into contact with the Lesser Bird of Paradise. The two sub-species involved in this instance are *Paradisea minor finschi* and *Paradisea raggiana salvadorii*. It is apparent that interbreeding between these closely related birds takes place fairly freely wherever they meet and specimens, recognised and unrecognised, probably exist in many museums. There is a skin at the British Museum (Natural History) and the type specimen, formerly in the Rothschild Collection at Tring, Hertfordshire, is at the American Museum of Natural History, New York, together with one other.

Just as *Paradisea mixta's* gracing of the list of legitimate species was destined to be short-lived (nine years), so too was Errol Flynn's flirtation with the birds of paradise and the natural history of New Guinea:

> My boys and I had reached the banks of the Sepik River. There seemed no possible way to get over it. It was broad and turbulent and full of crocodiles.
>
> I had my boys build a bamboo raft. When it was done, we put all of my birds of paradise carcasses, preserved in salt, on board. I packed everything else I owned: money, guns, binoculars, rolled tobacco, waxed matches, equipment, gear.
>
> We shoved off and headed towards the rapids below us, and the flats just beyond that . . . we went along miraculously for a time, and were getting near the flats, when we ran on to a pinnacle of rocks.

Figure 47
A Sepik River 'spirit house'
photographed in the 1890s. Errol
Flynn would have passed many
buildings like this during his New
Guinea adventures.

PARADISEA MIXTA

The crash split the raft apart. All of us went into the water – my six Kanakas and I – and we were rushed over boiling falls. We landed on the flats – but minus everything. All of it was washed away, birds of paradise, feathers, plumage, salt and all.

And that is just about where we came in!

LUPTON'S BIRD OF PARADISE

Paradisea raggiana × *Paradisea apoda*

Paradisea apoda luptoni Lowe, 1923, *Bulletin of the British Ornithologists' Club*, 43, p.10.
Paradisea apoda novae-guineae × *Paradisea apoda salvadorii* Mayr, 1941, *List of New Guinea Birds*, p.181.

DESCRIPTION

Lores and chin black glossed green; throat iridescent bottle green; rest of head and neck yellow with narrow but distinct yellow collar wrapping around beneath green of throat; velvet blackish brown breast cushion; lower breast and abdomen lighter brown; back, wings and tail darker brown; flank plumes vivid orange becoming more cinnamon towards tips; central retrices long and wire-like.

MEASUREMENTS

Length (excluding plumes) 360 mm (14 inches); wing 195 mm; tail 145 mm; bill 36 mm; tarsus 50 mm.

PLACE OF ORIGIN

Upper Fly River, southern New Guinea.

LOCATION OF SPECIMENS

London (Tring).

Plate XXXXI
Lupton's Bird of Paradise. Oil
painting by Mary Philcox.

Lupton's Bird of Paradise

As the nineteenth century drew to a close and fashions steadily changed, so too did attitudes to wild birds. In North America, parts of Europe, in Australia, New Zealand and a few other outposts of the British Empire, societies sprang up with the express intention not just of studying birds but of protecting them. Even at this surprisingly early period some of these organisations achieved considerable power, and during the first decades of the twentieth century some remarkably stringent legislation was introduced to facilitate bird protection. Quite naturally, this legislation was mostly aimed at safeguarding the birds of the particular country in which the society operated, but some attempts at protection on an international scale were made. Commercial plume-hunting in New Guinea, for instance, was outlawed and the plume trade was effectively ended by laws banning the importation of bird of paradise skins to those countries that had, formerly, been major importers. The United States was the first country to introduce such legislation (under the Wilson Tariff Act of 1913) but other nations, once World War I was over, quickly followed suit.

It is probable, however, that changing fashions had more to do with the cessation of large-scale hunting operations than did the new laws, for the fact is that paradise

plumes had long ceased to be high fashion items and were increasingly perceived as rather gross ornamentations, in much the same way as fur coats are regarded today.

Figure 49
Part of the same seizure arranged in even more bizarre fashion.

As the plume trade stuttered to a halt, customs officers around the world occasionally confiscated hauls of bird of paradise skins. One of the most spectacular took place at Laredo, Texas on 29 January, 1916 when 527 skins of the Greater Bird of Paradise (*Paradisea apoda*) were taken from one Abraham Kallman. Mr. Kallman was fined the, then, very considerable sum of $2,500 and imprisoned for six months for his customs offence. Perhaps the most remarkable aspect of the whole affair was the extraordinary photography that commemorated the event.

A few years later a smaller, but possibly more interesting, confiscation was made at Newhaven in Sussex, England. Here, on 25 February 1923, a box containing approximately sixty bird of paradise skins from the Merauke district of southern New Guinea was noticed and then taken by officers of His Majesty's Customs. When critically examined at the British Museum these skins were found to differ from the more usual specimens of plume birds. Dr Lowe, an ornithologist working at the Museum, considered the differences sufficiently marked to warrant naming a new sub-species of the Greater Bird of Paradise and proposed *Paradisea apoda luptoni* in honour of a Mr A.S. Lupton of H.M. Customs and Excise. In his description of the birds Lowe acknowledged that separate naming might be inappropriate, excusing himself in the following manner:

> The name is based solely on colouration, and is bestowed in order to call attention to what may be an interesting instance of hybridism, the colour of the pectoral plumes being 'clocked egg' . . . that is to say exactly intermediate between *P.a. raggiana* and *P.a. novaeguineae*.

Plate XXXXII
(Next page): Count Raggi's Bird of Paradise (*Paradisea raggiana*). Hand-coloured lithograph by J. Wolf and J. Smit from D.G. Elliot's *Monograph of the Paradiseidae* (London, 1873), Pl.2.

Plate XXXXIII
(Page 131), Greater Bird of Paradise (*Paradisea apoda*) – male left, female right. Hand-coloured lithograph by J. Wolf and J. Smit from D.G. Elliot's *Monograph of the Paradiseidae* (London, 1873), Pl.1.

J. Wolf & J. Smit del. et lith.

M & N. Hanhart imp

PARADISEA RAGGIANA.

J. Wolf. & J. Smit del. et lith.

M & N. Hanhart

PARADISEA APODA.

According to Walter Rothschild this was not the first time that such birds had come to the attention of ornithologists, the earliest recorded specimens having been taken on the Fly River in 1877 by the Italian explorer Signor Luigi Maria d'Albertis. D'Albertis's book, *New Guinea: What I Did and What I Saw* (1880), is one of the great eccentricities of New Guinea travel literature. An impressive result of his bravery and keen power of observation, it is also a catalogue of his colourful, and splendidly arrogant, behaviour. On his Fly River journey he had obtained a series of birds showing various intergradations of plumage between the Greater Bird of Paradise (*Paradisea apoda*) and Count Raggi's (*Paradisea raggiana*). Some showed the unmixed red plumes of *raggiana* but lacked its yellow shoulder bar; others had this shoulder bar but displayed plumes of a colour closer to *apoda's*. Rothschild's point was, presumably, that at least one of d'Albertis's birds was identical to *luptoni* and that Lowe's specimens could therefore be matched with that series. This implies that the Greater Bird of Paradise and Count Raggi's breed freely together in those areas where their ranges overlap (along the Fly River) and that their hybrids display various combinations of the parents' plumage characteristics. Probably, *luptoni* is simply one among a series of random intergradations, for almost certainly any hybrids produced retain fertility and thus smudge the issue considerably.

Figure 50
(Left), Luigi Maria d'Albertis ascending the Fly River in his boat, the *Neva*.

Figure 51
(Right), The Italian explorer Luigi Maria d'Albertis (1841–1901).

It might be added that there is no general agreement regarding the precise relationship of Count Raggi's Bird of Paradise and the Greater Bird of Paradise to each other. Some authorities consider them a single species (Count Raggi's birds representing several sub-species of the Greater), others keep them separate, but however the classification is made, they remain very closely related birds. Lupton's Bird of Paradise can therefore be seen either as a cross between sub-species, or as a hybrid of birds that are just barely differentiated into two species.

The type specimen – reg. no. 1923.3.1.1 – is at the British Museum (Natural History) together with other examples. Possibly, specimens exist in several other museums.

FRAU REICHENOW'S BIRD OF PARADISE

Paradisea raggiana × *Paradisea guilielmi*

Paradisea maria Reichenow, 1894, *Orn. Monatsber.*, 2, p.22.

Paradisea duivenbodei Menegaux, 1913, *Rev. Franc. Orn.,* 5, p.49.

Paradisea apoda augustae-victoriea × *Paradisea guilelmi* Stresemann, 1930, *Novitates Zoologicae*, 36, p.9.

Paradisea minor finschi × *Paradisea guilelmi* Stresemann, 1930, *Novitates Zoologicae*, 36, p.9.

DESCRIPTION

Forehead, cheeks, throat and front half of crown metallic green; rear of head and nape yellow looping round to form a distinct collar beneath green of throat; back and lesser wing coverts yellow; greater wing coverts brown washed yellow; tail, remainder of wings and underparts brown with a distinct lilac-hued brown breast pad; tail coverts yellow in *maria* brown in *duivenbodei*; ornamental flank plumes white mixed with rusty reddish brown giving overall rose, grey and violet appearance in *maria*, more yellow in *duivenbodei*.

MEASUREMENTS

Length (excluding plumes) 360 mm (14 inches); wing 185 mm; tail 140 mm; bill 33 mm; tarsus 45 mm.

PLACE OF ORIGIN

Mountains of the Huon Peninsula, Papua New Guinea; Yaour (Jaur), Geelvink Bay, Irian Jaya?

LOCATION OF SPECIMENS

P. maria: Berlin – two specimens? New York – four specimens. *P. duivenbodei*: Paris.

Plate XXXXIV
Frau Reichenow's Bird of Paradise
(right) with female Emperor of
Germany's Bird of Paradise
(*Paradisea guilielmi*). Oil painting by
Errol Fuller.

Frau Reichenow's Bird of Paradise

In 1894 the skin of an unusual but very beautiful plumed bird of paradise from the Finisterre Mountains was brought to the attention of Professor Anton Reichenow, Director of the Berlin Museum. Although primarily a specialist in African birds, Professor Reichenow had more than a passing interest in birds of paradise and he at once realised that the specimen before him was unlike any plume bird he had previously seen. Possibly for reasons of domestic diplomacy, more probably out of genuine feeling, Professor Reichenow named what he believed to be a new, and exquisite, species after his wife Maria. Walter Rothschild, with his very particular interest in birds of paradise, was immediately alerted to the new find but he, uncharacteristically, was sceptical of Reichenow's bird and suggested that it might be a hybrid. Nevertheless, Rothschild's collecting zeal was aroused and he did his best to secure an example for his own museum, but it was sixteen years before a similar bird became available. In due course it arrived at the Rothschild Zoological Museum to be followed – almost, it seems, inevitably – by another a year later (1911). Rothschild's unrelenting acquisitional instincts were to result in two further specimens falling into his hands, while the Berlin Museum managed to obtain yet another to lie alongside the one they had acquired in 1894.

During 1913, Monsieur A. Menegaux, an ornithologist at the Muséum d'Histoire Naturelle, Paris, published a description of an almost identical bird under the name *Paradisea duivenbodei*, a name given in honour of Renesse van Duivenbode, the Dutch merchant connected with the discovery of a number of problematical birds of paradise. *Paradisea duivenbodei* was examined, almost at once, by Rothschild who pronounced it inseparable from Reichenow's *Paradisea maria*. Certainly both forms could be distinguished from all other members of the genus *Paradisea* by the combination of lightly coloured flank plumes, a green skull cap and a distinct yellow collar. With the enthusiasm and generosity that were fairly typical of him, Rothschild loaned his specimens of *maria* to the Paris Museum for direct comparison. This enabled Menegaux to detail a number of small differences, the main points of these being that in *duivenbodei* the upper tail coverts are brown rather than straw yellow and the plumes more yellow than rusty red, slight differences that introduce discrepancies into an otherwise straightforward issue.

'*Paradisea maria*' is almost certainly a hybrid, and when Stresemann (1930) assembled his list of crosses he suggested the Emperor of Germany's Bird of Paradise (*Paradisea guilielmi*) and Count Raggi's Bird of Paradise (*Paradisea raggiana augustae-victoriae*) as the parents. Their plumage characteristics are quite evident in *maria* and, where their ranges overlap, altitudinal replacement of Count Raggi's Bird by the Emperor of Germany's occurs at heights above 2,275 feet (700 metres) bringing the two species into contact along fairly narrow fronts. The somewhat sketchy locality data accompanying the specimens is additional, and crucial, support for this theory, for one of the supposed parents, *guilielmi*, is known only from a very restricted area: the mountains of the Huon Peninsula. Four of the known skins were taken in these mountains, the fifth came without locality data, and a sixth is alleged to have come from the nearby Herzog Range. The label data for four birds now at the American

Figure 52
A ridge in the Finisterre Range. The
type specimen of *Paradisea maria*
was taken in these mountains.

Museum of Natural History (ex-Rothschild Collection) is curious in that it reflects
the changing, and conflicting, opinions that have been expressed in regard to them:

1. Purchased from agent in Berlin 1910, said to be from Sattleberg, but this is
doubtless an error. (Herzog Range?)

2. Purchased from Fritsche in Bremerhaven. Said to be from Sattleberg in 1911,
but this is doubtless an error. (Herzog Range?)

3. Came over with trade skins in 1921. Locality of course unknown but *P. maria*
with certainty only known from the Herzog Mts and said to be Finisterre Mts.

4. Sattleberg Mts. (Rec'd from Fritsche)

Figure 53
Papuans hunting plume birds.
Engraving by T.W. Wood from A.R.
Wallace's *Malay Archipelago*
(London, 1869).

Plate XXXXV
Emperor of Germany's Bird of
Paradise (*Paradisea guilielmi*) – male
above, females below. Hand-
coloured lithograph by W. Hart
from R. Bowdler Sharpe's *Monograph
of the Paradiseidae* (London, 1891–8),
Pl.27.

There is little reason to suppose the Sattleberg locality other than correct wherever it is alleged.

The origin of *Paradisea duivenbodei* is rather less certain, even though the only known example is recorded, quite precisely, as having been killed 'près de Yaour, dans la baie de Geelvink'. Rothschild's opinion that *duivenbodei* is a synonym for *maria* and that both are hybrids involving the action of the Emperor of Germany's Bird of

Paradise is not acceptable if a Geelvink Bay locality is acknowledged as reliable, for the area is several hundreds of miles from the Huon Peninsula, the alleged parent bird's only known home. Rothschild himself queried the locality almost immediately. As a result of this, Menegaux appears to have contacted Duivenbode who felt able to reaffirm – on what grounds it is not known – that the bird had definitely been taken near to Yaour. This locality (probably what is now known as Waar, an island just off the coast) seems to have been something of a regular purchasing place for Duivenbode: at least one other of his finds (the second specimen of Duivenbode's Six-wired Bird) had this particular place of origin. The spot where the merchant acquired his trade skins does not necessarily correspond to the spot where these were killed, however. Plume birds might, conceivably, have been transported for hundreds of miles, and passed through any number of Papuan hands along the way, before the Dutchman or his representatives got them. The actual place where any particular bird died was, presumably, of little importance to native traders.

Duivenbode's confirmation of locality was not enough, therefore, to satisfy Rothschild or, later, Stresemann, both of whom believed this claimed location to be false. Their decision was certainly judicious but it has been echoed as a proven fact. Mayr, in Peters (1962), lists *duivenbodei* with the following locality entry:

Near Jaur, Geelvink Bay (error), probably back of Astrolabe Bay.

By removing the given location and gratuitously substituting Astrolabe Bay (adjacent to the Huon Peninsula) it becomes possible to consider again the Emperor of Germany's Bird as a parent. Stresemann did just this in his influential essay of 1930. He remained worried by the differences between *duivenbodei* and *maria* that had been noticed by Menegaux some sixteen years earlier, and to account for these suggested that *duivenbodei* was the hybrid of the Lesser Bird of Paradise (*Paradisea minor finschi*) and the Emperor of Germany's (thereby excluding Count Raggi's from the cross). This is probably correct although differences between the forms might be explained by considering that the one kind represents the reciprocal cross to the other (i.e. male *raggiana* × female *guilielmi* as opposed to female *raggiana* × male *guilielmi*). Stresemann used this particular idea to explain quite significant differences between other problematical specimens (Elliot's Bird of Paradise and the Astrapian Sicklebill; the King of Holland's Bird of Paradise and the Lyre-tailed King) and it seems odd that he did not propose it as a possible alternative in this case. Certainly, the nature of *duivenbodei's* plumage argues slightly in favour of Stresemann's diagnosis, but this, of course, need not be conclusive.

Several possibilities can be considered in an evaluation of these forms. *P. maria* and *P. duivenbodei* could represent a single species, perhaps with two widely separated populations. This idea may or may not assume acceptance of the Yaour locality, but in either case it must be considered highly improbable. Another possibility is that the Emperor of Germany's Bird of Paradise has a population, apparently overlooked, existing hundreds of miles from the familiar one, and that this population occasionally interbreeds with the Lesser Bird of Paradise (Count Raggi's does not occur near to Geelvink Bay). This possibility is as unlikely as the last. By far the most realistic view is to accept the Yaour data as erroneous, to allow that *maria* and *duivenbodei* originate from the Huon Peninsula area and assume that both are hybrids of the birds that occur there.

The type of *maria*, from the Finisterre Mountains, and another allegedly taken in the Herzog Range were deposited in the Berlin Museum. The four examples that once belonged to Walter Rothschild are now part of the collection of the American Museum of Natural History, New York. Menegaux's *duivenbodei* has stayed in Paris.

CAPTAIN BLOOD'S BIRD OF PARADISE

Paradisea raggiana × *Paradisea rudolphi*

Paradisea bloodi Iredale, 1948, *Australian Zoologist*, 2, p.161.

DESCRIPTION

Head rusty orange brown; lores, chin and upper throat iridescent turquoise, violet and green with orange brown of head looping beneath to form a band separating throat from dark greyish brown breast cushion; abdomen greyish brown; wings greyish brown sheened olive green on upper wing coverts; back yellowish olive green; back of plumes rusty red, front slightly redder; tail brown; central retrices elongated (similar to *rudolphi*), coloured black, sheened with turquoise; iris brown; beak blue.

MEASUREMENTS

Length (excluding plumes) 310 mm (12 inches); wing 178 mm; tail 130 mm; bill 32 mm; tarsus 40 mm.

PLACE OF ORIGIN

Minyip, Mount Hagen.

LOCATION OF SPECIMEN

Sydney.

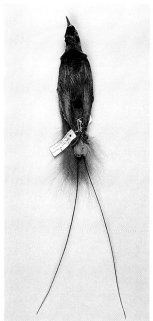

Plate XXXXVI
(Left), Captain Blood's Bird of
Paradise. Oil painting by Errol
Fuller.

Plates XXXXVII
and XXXXVIII (Top right and
above right), The unique specimen
of Captain Blood's Bird of Paradise
(underside top, upper parts below).
Courtesy of the Australian Museum,
Sydney.

Captain Blood's Bird of Paradise

It was after viewing the case of stuffed Birds of Paradise in the Natural History Museum that I was first stirred with the intense desire of seeing alive a Blue Bird of Paradise.

Thus did the adventures of Englishmen begin in the far-off days before the Great War. This particular adventure belonged to Sir William Ingram, *Bart.*, although, very properly, he was to take no active part in it. One Stalker was hired to undertake the long and arduous search for an almost legendary bird while Sir William confined himself to waiting at home and eventually immortalising the trip in the pages of *The Avicultural Magazine* for 1908.

After his comfortably matter-of-fact, yet curiously intimate, beginning Sir William soon adopted the entirely suitable tone of a *Boy's Own* paper. In darkest New Guinea . . .

Stalker had recovered from his illness and . . . started . . . for the interior . . . with ten natives, skilled in capturing live birds, and when at last he . . . reached the locality where the Blue Bird might be found he was confronted with the most serious obstacle he had yet met. His native followers refused to go into the bush . . . as they had learnt that the chief of the district had threatened to 'eat them up' if he caught them. There was only one alternative to returning empty-handed with all the labour of months wasted, and that was to beard the Lion in his Den. I am glad to say that Stalker, who is a plucky little Englishman, chose the latter and, with only an interpreter, boldly went into the chief's village and demanded a palaver. At first the Potentate refused to believe Stalker's assurance that they had come . . . simply to catch a live bird; and it was only after he was told that there was a great white chief who had more white warriors than there were trees in the forest, who desired to see a live specimen of this particular bird, and had told Stalker to get one, and had sent as a present to the chief a splendid tomahawk, that he was induced to give his consent to strangers hunting in his province.

History does not relate what eventually became of plucky little Stalker, but his blue bird of paradise died in its cage at the Regent's Park Zoo just three weeks after its arrival. Sir William Ingram, *Bart.*, moved on to an even more ambitious bird of paradise adventure. Convinced of the imminent extinction of the Greater Bird of Paradise (*Paradisea apoda*) he purchased the Caribbean island of Little Tobago, declared it a bird sanctuary, had almost fifty birds shipped from New Guinea to the West Indies, and then released them.

The wonderful Blue Bird of Paradise was first brought to the attention of naturalists in 1884. In that year the explorer Karl Hunstein plunged into uncharted cannibal-infested jungle, accompanied by just a single native boy, and emerged with this most exotic of all paradise birds. Fittingly, perhaps, it was named after a prince, and

one with the most romantic of associations. In their initial description Otto Finsch and A.B. Meyer, two German naturalists, named it *Paradisea rudolphi* in honour of Crown Prince Rudolph of Austria whom they describe as 'a protector of ornithological researches the world over'. Whatever the Prince's ornithological efforts, they have been largely forgotten. Today he is chiefly remembered for the romantic tragedy of his death at Mayerling where, together with his lover, he committed suicide.

His totally unforgettable bird is renowned not just for its breathtakingly beautiful appearance but also for its pulsating upside-down display in which the whole of the plumage is made to shimmer and shiver to the accompaniment of a wild, alien series of buzzes, shrieks and hums. It might be thought that this distinctive and altogether remarkable display would act as a sharp brake on any potential mating with less flamboyant species. That this is not always so, and that Prince Rudolph's Blue Bird of Paradise sometimes forgets its glorious dignity, is indicated by a single bird brought back from jungle patrol on 20 September 1944 by Captain Neptune (Ned) Blood.

Like many bold predecessors, including, of course, Hunstein and Stalker, Captain Blood penetrated what was then virtually virgin territory. Operating at the now well-known northern end of the Wahgi Valley, he collected a very strange male bird in adult plumage at Minyip, Mount Hagen. This amazing creature stands so well in appearance between Prince Rudolph's Blue Bird and Count Raggi's Bird of Paradise

Figure 54
(Left), Crown Prince Rudolph of Austria (1858–89).

Figure 55
(Right), Sir William Ingram.

(*Paradisea raggiana*) that there is little doubt as to its origin. The head is a rusty orange brown, the throat a combination of turquoise, violet and green, the breast and wings are greyish brown and the plumes are rusty red.

Blood was in the habit of making collections of birds of paradise during his patrols and established, with help from Sir Edward Hallstrom, an aviary station at Nondugl. From here, for a number of years, he supplied zoos and aviaries the world over, while his research material was sent mostly to the Australian Museum in Sydney. It was to this institution that he forwarded his most remarkable find, and it is here that it remains to this day (museum no.037682). It fell to Tom Iredale, a zoologist working at the Museum, to publish an initial description. Not quite able to bring himself to regard the mysterious bird as a hybrid, he described it as a species and named it *Paradisea bloodi*.

Although it is difficult to envisage the circumstances under which the extraordinary and aberrant Blue Bird would pair with an individual of another species, certain exceptional, but quite definable, conditions may have combined to bring this about. Prince Rudolph's Bird of Paradise is a species fast disappearing wherever it comes into contact with modern man. The very forests where Captain Blood made his find have, in the last few decades, been increasingly replaced by grasslands and the Blue Bird appears unable to adapt to changing conditions. The primary forest that does remain in this area now lies largely above 6,500 feet (2,000 metres), a height that is above the altitudinal limits of the species. E.T. Gilliard (1969) described how individuals were being trapped in small peninsulas of forest that were left, here and here, jutting down from the heights above into the ever encroaching grasslands. Here, isolated blue birds were coming into contact with the abundant, and seemingly much more adaptable, Count Raggi's Bird of Paradise, individuals of which species were thrusting up from below. Gilliard's point, that man may inadvertently have shattered the isolating mechanisms operating between these species, perhaps provides the best explanation for Captain Blood's amazing bird.

It is surprising to find, however, that another, and even more startling, allegation has been made against Prince Rudolph's Bird. The Australian ornithologist Richard Schodde has suggested that a bird – very similar to the female of Lawes' Six-wired Bird of Paradise (*Parotia lawesi*) – collected by R. Bulmer on 15 February 1956 at Trepikama in the Baiyer Valley and now at the Australian Museum (no.040100) may be a hybrid of Lawes' Six-wired and the Blue Bird. Apart from lacking a pale stripe on the cheeks, possessing a more richly coloured breast and showing slight purple sheening on the head, the bird appears identical to other Lawes' six-wired females. It is difficult to interpret quite what these slight differences mean, and the grounds for connecting them with Prince Rudolph's Bird of Paradise might not seem particularly firm. However, there is little doubt that a peculiar relationship does exist between Lawes' Bird and Prince Rudolph's. William Peckover (1990) has pointed out the strange fact that blue birds appear to choose display trees situated directly above the dance 'arenas' of six-wired birds.

One observation can, perhaps, be made. The bird known as *Paradisea bloodi* provides the proof that Prince Rudolph's Blue Bird has crossed with Count Raggi's. If the Blue illicitly mates with individuals of other bird of paradise species, then some truly marvellous creatures must sometimes flit through Papuan mountain forests.

Plate XXXXIX
Prince Rudolph's Bird of Paradise
(*Paradisea rudolphi*). Oil painting by
Errol Fuller.

146

Figure 56
Captain Neptune Blood watching
his daughter Susan entertaining a
group of highlanders from the Jimi
River area (Captain Blood is
standing immediately behind his
daughter).

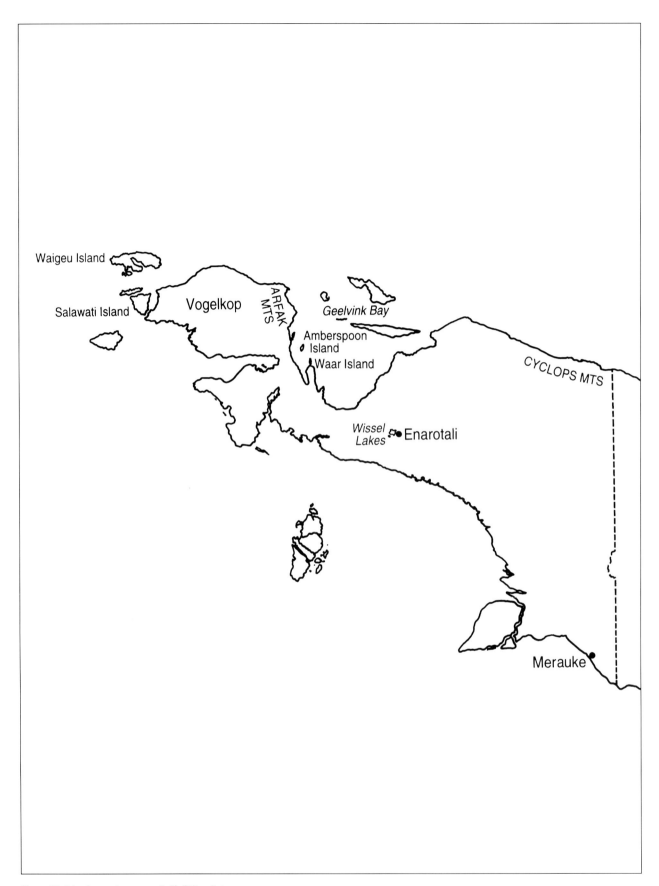

Figure 57: Irian Jaya – the western half of New Guinea.

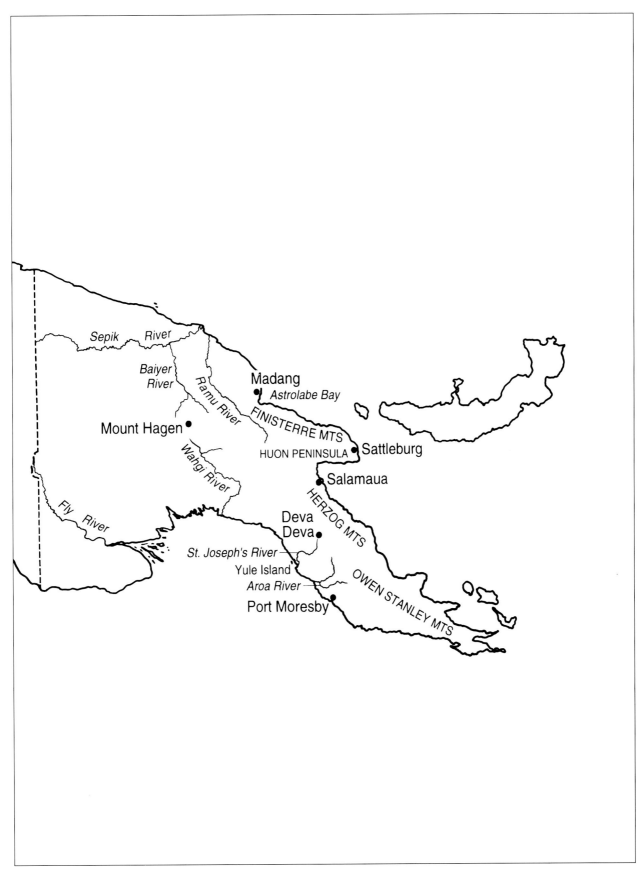

Figure 58: Papua – the eastern half of New Guinea.

ACKNOWLEDGEMENTS

The author would like to thank these people for their help: Warren Anderson, Brenda Ball, Sol Benn, Peter Blest, Walter Boles, Siegfried Eck, René Dekker, I.C.J. Galbraith, Ray Harris-Ching, Emma Hawkins, Mary LeCroy, Audrey Lomas, Anne Love, Alistair McAlpine, G.F. Mees, John Metcalf, Pat Morris, Shane Parker, Nick Peters, Miriam Rothschild, Michael Walter, Michael Walters, Derrick Witty.

BIBLIOGRAPHY

Beehler, B.M., 'Lek behaviour of the Lesser Bird of Paradise', *Auk*, 100: 992–5 (1983).

Bergman, S., 'On the display and breeding of the King Bird of Paradise, *Cicinnurus regius rex* (Scop.), in captivity', *Nova Guinea*, 7, part 2: 197–205 (1956).

Bock, W.J., 'Relationships between the birds of paradise and the bower birds', *Condor*, 65 (2): 91–125 (1963).

Coates, B.J., *The Birds of Papua New Guinea*, 2 vols, Dove Publications, Alderley, Queensland (1985–90).

Cooper, W.T. and Forshaw, J.M., *The Birds of Paradise and Bowerbirds*, Collins, Sydney (1977).

Cory, C.B., *The Beautiful and Curious Birds of the World*, Boston (1880–3).

D'Albertis, L.M., *New Guinea: What I Did and What I Saw*, 2 vols, Sampson Low, London (1880).

D'Albertis, L.M. and Salvadori, T., 'Catalogo degli uccelli raccolti da L.M. D'Albertis durante la 2ᵃ e 3ᵃ esplorazione del Fiume Fly negli anni 1876 e 1877', *Ann. Mus. Civ. Genova*, 14, ser. 1: 21–147 (1879).

Dharmakumarsinhji, Prince K.S., 'Notes on the breeding of the Empress of Germany's Bird of Paradise in captivity', *Zoologica*, 28, part 3: 139–44 (1943).

Diamond, J.M., 'Preliminary results of an ornithological exploration of the North Coastal Range, New Guinea', *American Museum Novitates* no. 2362: 1–57 (1969); 'Avifauna of the Eastern Highlands of New Guinea', *Publications of the Nuttall Ornithological Club* no. 12: 1–438, Cambridge, Mass. (1972); 'Rediscovery of the Yellow-fronted Bowerbird', *Science*, 216: 431–4 (1982).

Dinsmore, J.J., 'History and natural history of *Paradisea apoda* on Little Tobago Island, West Indies', *Caribbean Journal of Science*, 10: 93–100 (1970).

Downham, C.F., *The Feather Trade: A Case for the Defence*, London Chamber of Commerce, London (1910).

Elliot, D.G., *A Monograph of the Paradiseidae*, London (1873).

Everett, M., *The Birds of Paradise and Bowerbirds*, New Burlington Books, London (1980).

Everitt, C., 'Breeding the Magnificent Bird of Paradise', *Avicultural Magazine*, 71: 146–8 (1965).

Finsch, O. and Meyer, A.B., 'On some new Paradise birds' (translation of article, 1885), *Zeitschr. Ges. Orn.*), *Ibis*, ser. 5, 4: 237–58 (1886).

Flynn, E., *My Wicked, Wicked Ways*, William Heinemann, London (1960).

Frith, C.B., 'Display of Count Raggi's Bird of Paradise *Paradisea raggiana* and congeneric species', *Emu*, 81: 193–201 (1981).

Frith, D.W. and Frith, C.B., 'Courtship display of the Superb Bird of Paradise *Lophorina superba*', *Emu*, 88: 183–8 (1988).

Frost, W.J.C., 'The nesting habits of the King Bird of Paradise', *Avicultural Magazine*, ser. 4, 8: 33–5 (1930).

Fuller, E., 'Hybridisation amongst the Paradiseidae', *Bulletin of the British Ornithologists' Club*, 99 (4): 145–52 (1979).

Gilliard, E.T., *Birds of Paradise and Bower Birds*, Weidenfeld and Nicolson, London (1969).

Gould, J. and Sharpe, R.B., *The Birds of New Guinea*, 5 vols, London (1875–88).

Gray, A.P., *Bird Hybrids – A Checklist with Bibliography*, Commonwealth Agricultural Bureaux, Farnham Royal, Buckinghamshire, England (1958).

Hartert, E., 'Types of birds in the Tring Museum', *Novitates Zoologicae*, 25: 129 (1919).

Healey, C.J., 'Communal display of Princess Stephanie's Astrapia *Astrapia stephaniae* (Paradiseidae)', *Emu*, 78: 197–200 (1978).

Hornaday, W.T., *The Statement of the Permanent Wild Life Protection Fund, 1915–16*, vol. 2, published by the Fund, New York (1916).

Ingram, Sir W., 'Prince Rudolph's Bird of Paradise', *Avicultural Magazine* (December): 60–4 (1908).

Iredale, T., *Birds of Paradise and Bower Birds*, Georgian House, Melbourne (1950).

Junge, G.C.A., 'Zoological Results of the Dutch New Guinea Expedition, 1939', no. 5, *Zoological Verhandelingen, Leiden*, 20: 1–77 (1953).

Labillardière, J.J., *Voyage in Search of La Perouse*, London (1800).

LeCroy, M., 'The Genus *Paradisea* – Display and Evolution', *American Museum Novitates*, no. 2714: 1–52 (1981).

Mayr, E., *List of New Guinea Birds*, The American Museum of Natural History, New York (1941);
Systematics and the Origin of Species, Columbia University Press, New York (1942);
in Peters, J.L., *A Checklist of the Birds of the World*, vol. 15, Museum of Comparative Zoology, Cambridge, Mass. (1962).

Mayr, E. and Gilliard, E.T., 'The Ribbon-tailed Bird of Paradise (*Astrapia mayeri*) and its allies', *American Museum Novitates* no. 1551: 1–13 (1952).

Meek, A.S., *A Naturalist in Cannibal Land*, Fisher Unwin, London (1913).

Menegaux, A., 'Description de deux nouveaux Paradisiers (*Paradisea duivenbodei* et *P. ragg. sororia*)', *Revue. Franç. d'Orn.*, 5: 49–51 (1913);
'Sur l'hybridation dans le genre *Paradisea L.*, 1758', *Revue Franç. d'Orn.*, 4: 33–5 (1915).

Mitis, Baron von, *The Life of Crown Prince Rudolph of Habsburg*, Skeffington and Son, London (1930).

Ogilvie-Grant, W.R., 'Report on the birds collected by the British Ornithologists' Union Expedition and the Wollaston Expedition in Dutch New Guinea', *Ibis*, Jubilee Supp. no. 2 (1915).

Peckover, W.S., *Papua New Guinea Birds of Paradise*, Robert Brown, Carina, Queensland (1990).

Peckover, W.S. and Filewood, L.W.C., *Birds of New Guinea and Tropical Australia*, Reed, Sydney (1976).

Pratt, A.E., *Two Years Among New Guinea Cannibals*, Philadelphia (1906).

Pruett-Jones, S.G. and Pruett-Jones, M.A., 'A promiscuous mating system in the Blue Bird of Paradise *Paradisea rudolphi*', *Ibis*, 130: 373–7 (1988).

Rand, A.L., 'Results of the Archbold Expeditions, no. 22: On the breeding habits of some birds of paradise in the wild', *American Museum Novitates* no. 993: 1–8 (1938);
'Results of the Archbold Expeditions, no. 26: Breeding habits of the birds of paradise *Macgregoria* and *Diphyllodes*', *American Museum Novitates* no. 1073: 1–14 (1940).

Rand, A.L. and Gilliard, E.T., *Handbook of New Guinea Birds*, Weidenfeld and Nicolson, London (1967).

Ripley, S.D., 'A systematic and ecological study of birds of New Guinea', *Bulletin of the Peabody Museum of Natural History*, no. 19: 1–87 (1964).

Rothschild, L.W., *Das Tierreich*, lieferung 2 – *Aves Paradiseidae*, Friedländer und Sohn, Berlin (1898);
'On recently described Paradiseidae', *Ibis*: 353–4 (1911);
'Remarks on sporadic and racial hybrids', *Bulletin of the British Ornithologists' Club*, 43: 125–9 (1923);
'Remarks on birds of paradise known only from single examples', *Bulletin of the British Ornithologists' Club*, 50: 38–40 (1930).

Rothschild, L.W. and Hartert, E., 'Notes on Papuan Birds' *Novitates Zoologicae*, 10: 65–116; 196–231; 435–480 (1903).

Rothschild, M., *Dear Lord Rothschild*, Hutchinson, London (1983).

Rousseau-Decelle, G., 'Notes sur deux hybrides naturels de Paradisiers', *L'Oiseaux, N.S.*, 7: 240–5 (1937).

Schodde, R., 'Evolution in the birds of paradise and bowerbirds, a resynthesis', *In* Frith, H.J., and Calaby, J.H. (eds.), *Proc. Int. Ornith. Congr.* no. 16, Australian Academy of Science, Canberra (1976).

Schodde, R. and McKean, J.L., 'The species of the genus *Parotia* (Paradiseidae) and their relationships', *Emu*, 73: 145–56 (1973).

Sharpe, R.B., *Monograph of the Paradiseidae, or Birds of Paradise, and Ptilonorhynchidae, or Bower-Birds*, 2 vols, London (1891–8).

Sibley, C.G. and Ahlquist, J.E., *Phylogeny and Classification of Birds*, Yale University Press, New Haven (1991).

Sibley, C.G., Ahlquist, J.E. and Monroe, B.L., 'A classification of the living birds of the world based on DNA-DNA hybridisation studies', *Auk*, 105: 409–23 (1988).

Sibley, C.G. and Monroe, B.L., *Distribution and Taxonomy of Birds of the World*, Yale University Press, New Haven (1991).

Sims, R.W., 'Birds collected by Mr F. Shaw Mayer in the central highlands of New Guinea, 1950–1951', *Bulletin of the British Museum (Natural History)*, Zool., 3, no. 10 (1956).

Stonor, C.R., 'The evolution and mutual relationships of some members of the Paradiseidae', *Proceedings of the Zoological Society of London*, 106: 1177–85 (1938);
'A new species of paradise bird of the genus *Astrapia*', *Bulletin of the British Ornithologists' Club*, 59: 57–61 (1939);
Courtship and Display Among Birds, London (1940).

Stresemann, E., 'Die Heimat der *Paradisea maria* Reichenow', *Ornithologisch Monatsberichte*, 33: 128 (1925);
'Welche Paradiesvogelarten der Literatur sind Hybriden Ursprungs?', *Novitates Zoologicae*, 36: 6–15 (1930);
'Die Entdeckungsgeschichte de Paradiesvögel', *Journal für Ornithologie*, 95: 263–91 (1954);
Ornithology from Aristotle to the Present (translated by Epstein, H.J. and C.), Harvard University Press, Cambridge, Mass. (1975).

Suchetet, A., *Des hybrids à l'état sauvage. Règne animal*, tome premier, *Classe des Oiseaux*, Baillière et Fils, Paris (1877).

Ward, E., 'On a new species of Sicklebill', *Proceedings of the Zoological Society*: 742 (1873).

INDEX